PLANNING A YEAR'S PULPIT WORK

PLANNING A YEAR'S PULPIT WORK

ANDREW W. BLACKWOOD

BAKER BOOK HOUSE
Grand Rapids, Michigan

Library of Congress Catalog Card Number: 43-4033

© 1942 by Whitmore & Stone

Paperback Edition
issued July 1975 by
Baker Book House
with permission of copyright owner

ISBN: 0-8010-0640-6

First printing, July 1975
Second printing, April 1977

PHOTOLITHOPRINTED BY CUSHING - MALLOY, INC.
ANN ARBOR, MICHIGAN, UNITED STATES OF AMERICA
1 9 7 7

DEDICATED
TO THE
PASTORS AND STUDENTS
WHO HAVE
HELPED ME WRITE THIS BOOK

FOREWORD

THIS BOOK IS FOR THE PARISH MINISTER OR ADVANCED STUDENT OF theology. The emphasis is on "What to Preach," [1] and the content is largely Biblical. The ideals are much the same as in *Preaching from the Bible*,[2] but the emphasis is more on a popular teaching ministry.

The purpose is not to provide materials for next Sunday's sermons, or ready-made molds into which a minister can pour what he finds for himself. Anyone who desires that sort of "help" can secure it elsewhere, but in so doing he may lose some of life's holiest joys. The friends who handle religious books report that certain clergymen seem to rely largely on the printed discourses and outlines of other ministers. If so, there is likely to be plagiarism, which is stealing, and stealing is sin.

The present desire is to encourage original thinking. Ideally, it should be creative; more often it will be constructive. As for the homiletical patterns, they should vary from week to week. Under the guidance of the Holy Spirit, every man ought to work out his homiletical forms. Meanwhile there is need of a volume dealing with the content of a popular teaching ministry today.[3]

This book has grown out of personal experience. In no chapter is there any armchair theory. Some books about preaching are full of theories, as they ought to be; this one has more to do with facts. Out of his own experience as pastor and teacher—with constant aid from effective workers now on the field, including many former students—the writer has drawn every concrete proposal. Both

[1] Title of a strong book by H. S. Coffin, Doran, 1928; cf. A. B. Scott, *Preaching Week by Week*, Hodder & Stoughton, London, 1929.

[2] A. W. Blackwood, Abingdon-Cokesbury, 1941.

[3] See W. H. P. Faunce, *The Educational Ideal in the Ministry*, Macmillan, 1908; ch. i, "The Place of the Minister in Modern Life."

in the choice of materials and in the treatment of them the determining factor has been the needs of the parish minister today.

Whatever the denomination, the pastor of the local church should have a program for the year's pulpit work. In making his plans he ought to consider the state of the times, the needs of the congregation, and the bent of his mind. No young David should sally forth in King Saul's armor. Neither ought any man to be in bondage to a system, even though he has devised it himself. At a stage in world history when no one can tell what an hour will bring forth, even the best of human programs should be subject to revision, perhaps overnight.

Any such plan is for the study, not the pulpit. What the pastor does there should call no special attention to itself. To the friends before him the pulpit work ought to seem inspiring and helpful, rather than informative and heavy. However, the laymen should be aware that the minister works hard in the study, and that he is growing as a preacher. They ought to feel that back of every pulpit utterance there is solid reading, as well as quiet brooding, all in the spirit of prayer. They should be able to thank God for a pastor who speaks with authority as well as enthusiasm.

In short, this book is for the parish interpreter of the Christian religion. If he is to prove worthy of his office he must keep growing. In order to do that he ought to have a plan for conserving his time and energy. All the while he should keep humble. To that end he may put over his study desk as a motto the words of the foremost Christian preacher: "I count not myself to have apprehended; but this one thing I do, forgetting those things which are behind, and reaching forth unto those things which are before, I press toward the mark for the prize of the high calling of God in Christ Jesus." [4]

ANDREW WATTERSON BLACKWOOD

The Theological Seminary
Princeton, New Jersey.

[4] Phil. 3:13-14.

CONTENTS

A PRELIMINARY SURVEY

UNDERGIRDING

From September to Christmas

10

HEARTENING

From Pentecost to September

A PRELIMINARY SURVEY

Chapter I

MAKING THE PLAN

THE WISE MINISTER PREACHES ACCORDING TO A PROGRAM. HE
makes it himself and is free to change it at will. He thinks of
himself as a gardener who is appointed by the King to feed several
hundred people throughout the year. The gardener keeps a succession of plants growing in various beds. He can water them
all in the time that a novice would devote to a single corner.
What is more pleasing than a garden that is carefully planned as
well as nurtured? This homemade parable shows what one
means by a popular teaching ministry.

Almost every strong pastoral preacher has had some way of
planning his pulpit work. There is an impression that Beecher
or Spurgeon busied himself all week about other things and on
Saturday night prepared his morning sermon. Even if either
man had been a magician, whatever came out of his coat sleeve
would first have gone in, according to a careful plan. A conjurer
manages to have more than one trick ready for use, but neither
divine was a sleight-of-hand preacher. However quickly any
discourse came to its final form, the message was the product of
long, hard thinking, as well as reading, over a period of time.

Once a lay friend heard Beecher allude to a sermon that he
had in mind. After watching for weeks the layman inquired
what had happened to the message. Beecher replied that it was
still ripening in his garden. Months later when he delivered
that discourse it seemed extemporaneous. So it was, in literary
form, but not in substance. The best "impromptu speaking" is

15

usually the result of reading and thinking about a subject on which a man is finally able to speak with joyous abandon.

A living sermon matures slowly, but at length it may ripen quickly. In order to give each message time to develop, according to the spirit of life in its seed, the pastor should have in his homiletical garden sermons in various stages of growth. Herein lies the essence of a plan for pulpit work. As for methods in detail, they should depend on the personality of the preacher. Hence the proposals in this book are not for adoption wholesale. "Where the Spirit of the Lord is, there is liberty." [1]

On the other hand, freedom may result in license. According to a tradition, Beecher was spending part of his summer holiday in a village upstate. On the Lord's Day he went to the meeting-house, where he listened to a brilliant discourse by a young minister who had recently been graduated from the divinity school. After the benediction the visiting divine said to the young clergyman, "How long did it take you to prepare that message?"

"Oh, three or four hours yesterday afternoon."

"That is astounding. It took me twenty years."

"You must be Henry Ward Beecher. I am not ashamed to deliver a sermon that it took you twenty years to prepare."

Without pausing to admire in the young man anything except his gall, let us note that even a preaching genius has some way of planning for the pulpit. During those twenty years countless sermons must have been growing together in Beecher's garden. Fortunately, however, the parish minister or seminary student need not take as his model such a man of genius. The average pastor can learn more from a preacher who has "pulpit talent." For example, think of Charles E. Jefferson or Alexander McLaren. Each of them in his own fashion inspired a host of ministers who now work according to a plan made at home.

[1] II Cor. 3:17*b*.

Neither of those two masters, however, paid sufficient heed to the Christian Year.

THE BROAD PROGRAM

The simplest way to plan is to follow the calendar. That is the procedure in this book. First we shall consider a typical program as it relates to the morning sermon. Then we shall think about the preaching at the other services for which the pastor is responsible. There will be separate chapters concerning the most vital parts of the plan. Finally we shall look at the practical benefits to the minister and the people, as well as the possible disadvantages. All the while we shall stress the use of the Scriptures in meeting the practical needs of men today.

The best time to plan is during the summer vacation, when the minister is far enough away from the parish to see it as a whole. He can review the last year's pulpit work, and then think about what to do in the next twelve months. Gradually he can determine which crops to sow in the various fields. While an exceptional man is able to carry all these facts in his head, there can be no harm in putting them down on paper. Then the pastor can file his tentative program for reference, as well as revision.

Any such work sheet is for no eyes save those of the minister. Even his wife might think a homemade plan unworthy of her gifted husband. As for the lay officers, if they learned about their pastor's methods of preparing for the pulpit, they might become sermon-conscious, if not critical. However, they should be aware that he is a real student, even in midsummer. They should know that while he is resting his body up in the mountains he is filling his storehouse with spiritual food for his friends back at home.

The plan begins to operate in the autumn, which is "the

springtime of the Christian Year." A certain pastor is able to start early in September, whereas another prefers to wait until October. By that time nearly all the people will have returned from their vacations and the work should be well under way. It is wise to begin with a good deal of momentum.

The unit in planning is the quarter of the year. In any one case the period may be longer than three months, or else shorter. For instance, there are usually more than thirteen weeks between Christmas and Easter, and there are always fewer than thirteen between Easter and Pentecost. But for convenience we shall refer to each period as a quarter. This is one of many ways in which the minister should adapt his program to meet local conditions. Whatever the plan, it should be flexible.

In a city church it may be wise to proceed by the month. At present, however, it is easier to take three months as the unit of time. In a congregation where all the activities lead up to the quarterly communion, that is the goal towards which the preaching should look forward. Whatever the unit, the basic principles will become clear if one begins now to make a tentative plan for the pulpit work of the home church.

While there ought to be a broad program for the year, the detailed planning may be by the quarter. When the work starts in the fall, the minister should know in general what he is to do throughout the coming year, but he need concern himself only about the next three months. In fact, he may have at hand much of the material for the sermons during the coming quarter. If so, he can spend a good deal of his time during the autumn in preparing for the harvest season, which usually comes between Christmas and Easter. In such a cumulative way of working there are usually three months to make ready for what has not yet actually begun.

This is the ideal, but of course there are all sorts of exceptions.

Sometimes there are unavoidable interruptions. Meanwhile, one fact should be clear: however long a sermonic truth has been growing in a man's garden, he should leave everything there until a few days before he needs to use it in the pulpit. There is no suggestion that a minister prepare a lot of sermons in advance and then lay them away in cold storage.

In our hypothetical parish the minister is directly responsible for three services: Sunday morning, Sunday evening, and the midweek meeting. If any of these is missing, the work of planning is that much simpler. If a man is new in the work of preparing sermons regularly, planning for one a week may be no slight task. Fortunately, however, the ability to make a program for pulpit work grows through proper use.

Whatever the number of weekly gatherings, each of them should differ from everything else during the seven days. Seek variety! One reason many a layman attends only a single service is that he knows all the others will be much the same, and not so good. He picks out the one that he prefers. It may be morning worship. That provides the pattern for the evening service. It in turn may be like the program in the men's class, with opening and closing exercises, as well as a lay sermon. Much the same procedure marks the midweek meeting. Is it any wonder that such sameness fails to attract the modern man?

As in feeding a family, it is wise to arrange for different sorts of meals. This is especially true of the relation between the adult Bible classes and the morning sermon. After people have spent the better part of an hour thinking about a certain portion of the Bible, when they come to the sanctuary they should have a change of fare. If there needs to be any shifting of program to avoid duplication, the responsibility lies with the minister.

For example, the adult classes may follow the International Lessons. Before he draws up his tentative plan for the next year's preaching he should ascertain what ground the lessons are to cover, quarter after quarter. The information is to be had from any denominational publishing house. Whatever ground the lessons cover, there is always some other field that is full of materials for the pulpit.

If there is variety from service to service on Sunday, there should be continuity from Sunday morning to Sunday morning, and from Sunday evening to Sunday evening. Each service ministers to its own set of spiritual needs. This is especially true of Sunday morning, for attendance at eleven o'clock is largely a matter of habit. While there ought to be refreshing variety of pulpit fare, the teaching minister looks on each Sunday morning message as an integral part of a unified program.

At first these facts may seem complicated. If so, the fault is in the statement, for in actual use they prove to be simple. But the work requires a good deal of ability as well as time. There must be a broad program, and then there must be a detailed plan. All the while there must be synthesizing power—that is, the ability to see things in relation to each other and then put them together as a unified whole.

All of this is the ideal, to which no one ever attains. In order to watch the unfolding of the plan let us look at the program for Sunday mornings.

SUNDAY MORNING SERMONS

The most important event of the week ought to be the Sunday morning hour of worship. Just now we are thinking only of the sermon. In the eyes of the community the usefulness of the preacher depends mainly on his Sunday morning messages. During the period leading up to Christmas they should provide the basis for the year's pulpit work. The keynote here may be *Undergirding.* A good way to start is to preach about Old Testament characters, one after another, in relation to God. While those worthies differed from each other as much as stars in the sky, the men and women of the Old Testament were at heart like those who sit in the pews today. The method in view calls for the use of Biblical cases in meeting the soul needs of men today.

The interest of the hearer should grow from week to week. That is more likely to be the case if the man in the pulpit is following a course. By a "course" one means a number of consecutive Sunday morning sermons of the same general character, but announced only from week to week. If there were a carefully unified "series," that would usually come at the evening service. Except in a downtown church—or in a congregation which has no evening service—it is usually better to run a series at night, but there can never be too many good courses of Sunday morning sermons.

The effect of the pulpit work will be all the greater if the successive sermons come from a field that is fairly well defined. One way of limiting the scope is to preach for a number of weeks from a single book of the Bible—it may be Genesis or Exodus, Judges or First Samuel. Any such book provides more material for case studies than one can use between the opening of the public schools and the coming of Christmas. The choice of the Biblical field depends partly on what one did the year before, as well as on the state of the times.

The logical place to begin is with Genesis,[2] which has to do with God and the home. The emphasis is on the Lord's way of dealing with one man after another. Surely no preaching could be more timely today. According to the plan under review, however, the chosen field is Exodus, which concerns God and the nation. Even the least socially-minded of us needs to learn that

[2] See Blackwood, *Preaching from the Bible,* pp.75-78, 201-6.

the Lord has a plan for His people collectively, as well as one by one. Now that the World War II has fixed our gaze upon Egypt, the Book of Exodus should lead to many a gripping sermon.

Whatever the part of the Bible, each message ought to be about the Almighty. Throughout the autumn the sermons may well be about "The Meaning of God in Human Experience." In religion and life, here and in heaven, the underlying truth of our religion is the will of the Lord in His dealings with men. By drawing these messages from the experiences of God's children in times of hardship, the pastor can make each Sunday morning sermon inspiring and helpful.

Week after week the trail should draw nearer to Bethlehem. Early in December there may be a message or two about the Redeemer as foreshadowed in one of the prophetic books, such as Isaiah or Micah. As Christmas itself draws near, there is a call for preaching directly about the Incarnation. At this season there is an opportunity for evangelism, at least indirectly—

> No ear may hear His coming,
> But in this world of sin,
> Where meek souls will receive Him still,
> The dear Christ enters in.[3]

The plans for preaching after Christmas should be different, for every once in a while the good shepherd moves his flock into another pasture. Between Christmas and Easter the sermons may be from one of the Gospels, perhaps St. Luke. If so, during the autumn the minister should spend an hour or two each morning with the chosen book. Before winter comes, all the Biblical materials may be in hand. Week after week there may be only

---

[3] Phillips Brooks, "O Little Town of Bethlehem."

the need of putting them together so as to accomplish the end in view.

The idea is to make each sermon a complete unit, for the man who comes to church only once a month should receive a satisfying message from the heart of God. But the regular attendant may well be aware that the morning sermons until Easter will be from the Gospel According to Luke. The pulpit work will mean all the more if the layman reads the book day after day in his home. By verbally making the request for such reading, and by frequent reminders in the bulletin, the minister can promote the use of the Bible as it was written, book by book, and paragraph by paragraph.[4]

During this quarter the keynote is *Recruiting*. The plan is to guide the bearer in using his mother's Bible so as to believe in his mother's Saviour. In the pulpit the emphasis should be increasingly evangelistic; at the center of every sermon should be the Lord Jesus. Week after week the man in the pew should come closer and closer to Him. These messages ought to culminate in preaching about the Cross and the Resurrection.

Starting out with new zest after Easter, the minister can preach from the Book of Acts.[5] A year later he may choose to deal with the post-Resurrection interviews of our Lord with the disciples. This is the trail that we are to follow. The idea is to preach about the Living Christ until after Pentecost, and then to consider the ensuing Sundays as part of the summer season. During the seven weeks after Easter, which is the climactic day of the Christian Year, it should be possible to keep the friends close to the Living Christ. At this season the keynote for the pulpit work may be *Instructing*.

[4]See Julian P. Love, *How to Read the Bible,* Macmillan, 1940; Peter Green, *The Devotional Use of the Bible,* S.P.C.K., London, 1939; Anthony C. Deane, *How to Enjoy the Bible,* Doran, 1929.

[5] See Blackwood, *op. cit.,* pp. 119-22.

As for the days beyond Pentecost, the weather will be getting warm, and the people may become restive. Hence the call will be for messages of hope and cheer. The technical name for this type of preaching used to be "pastoral"; the newer label is the "life-situation sermon." Whatever the title, the purpose is to deal with the needs of the Christian soul in trouble. By entering heartily into the spirit of each message the pastor will find such pulpit work unexpectedly fruitful as well as fascinating. It will likewise do his own heart good. In fact, he may enjoy his summer preaching as much as that of any other season. The keynote during June and July is *Heartening*.

In early summer the easiest way to prepare for Sunday morning sermons may be to have a course from the Psalms. For each message after Pentecost it is fairly easy to find part of a psalm that will show how the Lord heals the soul that is sick. The reference here is to disorders in the life that is Christian, and not to deadly sins that separate from God. This kind of pulpit work may become so absorbing that the minister will start jotting down suggestions for much the same sort of thing twelve months later. Nowhere more than in early summer does planning ensure permanent dividends. Such is the report that comes from busy pastors near and far.

SUNDAY EVENING SERMONS

We have been thinking about the basic plan, which has to do with the Sunday morning sermons. In a sense, what we are now to consider is of secondary concern. No matter how many other services there may be during the week, none of them is so vital as that on Sunday morning. Indeed, not every local church has a second service on the Lord's Day, or a gathering for social worship during the week.

If the pastor is responsible for only a single hour of public worship during the seven days, he should find it relatively easy to plan his pulpit work. During a young minister's first year or two out on the field such a working schedule may be a godsend. Week after week, if he prepares for an hour of uplift in worship, as well as an edifying sermon, he may have his hands full. But in the course of time, after he has learned how to handle his new tools, and has planted all sorts of sermonic seed-thoughts in his homiletical garden, he may wish to meet with some of his friends at the church more often than once a week.

There is still something to be said for the evening service, or else vespers. In three successive parishes the lay officers assured the writer that it was impossible to get the people out for the second service. They had one, but it lived at a "poor, dying rate." In each case, while the evening gathering never did attract the majority of those who came to morning worship, it proved feasible to enlist many others who had no church home. In each of those parishes the second service became a spiritual asset. In many a field this may be the most fruitful sort of work among adults.

Especially in days of crisis there may be a call for more frequent opportunities to worship God in the sanctuary. In some communities it is necessary to make such provision for those who are not free to attend at eleven o'clock in the morning. According to the Detroit correspondent of *The Christian Century*, men and women who are obliged to work on the Lord's Day have been asking their home churches to arrange popular evening services for those who feel weary and jaded. While the war has raised far more issues than it can ever solve, it has at least taught some of us mortals that we need God and the Church.

In Washington, D.C., at the Lutheran Church of the Reformation, Oscar F. Blackwelder seems to regard the evening service as the crowning feature of the day's worship. In that downtown sanctuary every Lord's Day there are three hours of public worship, and in it all nothing overshadows the sermon. At eight-thirty in the morning the assistant minister is in charge; at eleven o'clock the pastor takes the service; and at eight in the evening he feels that he comes into his own. That evening service appears to be his pride and joy.

Whenever he confers with young ministers, Dr. Blackwelder stresses the evening service. He says that if the Protestant Church is to thrive there must be more frequent and varied opportunities on Sunday for the people to worship God and enjoy the preaching of His Word. This clergyman says that in the earthly life of our Lord some of the most moving experiences came at night, and that the best way to reach the modern Nicodemus and his sister is through the evening service.

In order to attract people at night, the pulpit fare should differ from that in the morning. In the other parts of public worship, also, the evening hour should have an atmosphere all its own. Those who attend the second service are likely to be more thoughtful than the friends who come in the morning, or it may be that the evening attendants are more rested physically. Consequently, the way is open for a popular teaching ministry. In order to do such pulpit work effectively, the pastor should be able to plan.

The most auspicious time of year to start holding evening services is in the early fall. Thus the new habit of attending church after dark will have time to become fixed before the approach of summer. During the months leading up to Christmas it should be possible to secure a hearing at night. When people learn that there is to be an inspiring sermon about a doctrinal subject, they will come to church. If they receive help, they will return a week later, and some of them will bring their friends.

After the holidays the same persons should enjoy a series of popular sermons, "What It Means to Be a Christian." While such messages are somewhat evangelistic, they are also doctrinal. In fact, the best soul-winning preaching is always doctrinal, at least indirectly. There is sure to be a reason why the hearer should do what the preacher asks. In the series now proposed, the successive sermons would have to do with a man's experiences in finding God, through Christ and His Cross.

Of course any minister could preach the doctrinal sermons in the morning and then have the biographical messages at night. That is what the writer would do if he wished to make the evening service especially attractive to young people. But many a wise pastor encourages the young folk, as well as the boys and girls, to be present regularly on Sunday mornings at eleven o'clock.

One reason for striving to enlist the young people and the children at the morning service is that the future of the Christian Church, under God, rests largely with those who are now young. If they form the habit of enthusiastic church attendance on Sunday morning, and if they keep up the practice through the years, they will constitute the nucleus of the local church after their fathers and mothers have fallen asleep. But if the young folk do not form such habits, wherein lies the hope for the parish church of tomorrow?

MIDWEEK BIBLE READINGS

In the plan for the year's work there should also be a place for the midweek service. Throughout the Chicago area of The Methodist Church, according to the local correspondent of *The Christian Century,* there is a renewal of emphasis on the midweek meeting. Evidently the pastors and the stewards have found that there is no way of caring adequately for the souls of

God's children without some kind of social worship between Sundays. While it may not prove feasible to resuscitate a service that has breathed its last, it should be possible to start some other kind of midweek gathering—it may be cottage meetings.

As with the Sunday evening service, the best season to begin holding midweek meetings is early in the fall, because attendance should be largely a matter of habit. It is even more a question of finding the uplift that comes through informal worship, and the soul-food that results from opening up the Scriptures. If the minister plans for meetings that will give the people what they need, and then works hard in the study, more than a few will respond. If he makes ready every week with the care that the occasion warrants, he will enjoy these hours of fellowship with his most spiritually-minded friends.

For a more extended discussion of the midweek service, look elsewhere.[6] The additional suggestions here are two. In days of distress and confusion there is much to be learned from a course of Bible readings in the First Epistle of Peter. Even more timely is the proposal to take up on Wednesday evenings the geography of Bible lands. During recent years the onrush of invading troops has caused the newspaper reader and the radio listener to think in turn about almost every locality that is prominent in the Scriptures. Day after day the horizon of the average man has been broadened, geographically, but has he learned to look on the Eastern world as it is in the eyes of God?

On Wednesday evenings during autumn the minister can help the congregation to become geographically-minded. If there were need of a slogan, as there is not, it might be "Let Our Church Go Geographical." Informally pastor and people can discuss the geography of the Holy Land, as well as of Mesopo-

___
[6] See Blackwood, *op. cit.,* chap. ix.

tamia and the Mediterranean world.[7]   After such a series of
friendly conversations about cities and seas long dear to the
Christian heart, it should prove easier to make the Bible seem
real and missions momentous.   By careful study of the facts,
both in the Bible and in the world atlas today, and by constant
use of the imagination, the minister can make clear how the sea
and the dry land, the city and the open countryside, have afforded the setting for the drama of redemption.

Where in world literature, for instance, is there such a thrilling
account of a storm at sea as in the twenty-seventh chapter of the
Acts?   The geographical allusions there sound like those in a
current issue of the *New York Times*.   The Biblical record, however, concerns the Living Christ and His power to shield human
souls from fear.   If God's people are to know and love His Holy
Book, they should likewise know and love His Holy Land.

The subject "Bible Landmarks in Today's Headlines" was
used recently by a neighboring pastor, who within a year has
brought to his new and difficult parish an infusion of life and
hope.   In many another place where conventional methods seem
to have failed, there is surely some way of presenting the truths
of God attractively.   The reference here is to both the midweek
meeting and the Sunday evening service, for as a rule the two
belong together.   With a few minor changes the arguments for
and against either service would apply equally well to the other.

The reason for stressing the matter now is that the effectiveness
of either gathering, under the good hand of God, depends largely
on the ability of the minister to plan this part of his work, and
then carry out his program.   Somehow or other he can devise
ways for meeting with his people in larger or smaller groups at

[7] See G. A. Smith, *The Historical Geography of the Holy Land*, Harper, 1932;
Sir William Ramsay, *St. Paul, the Traveller and the Roman Citizen*, 1901, and
The Church in the Roman Empire, 1911, Putnam.

The Christian Year	International S.S. Lessons	Sunday Morning Sermons — The Basic Plan	Sunday Evening Sermons	Midweek Bible Readings
September to Christmas — *Undergirding*	"Light from Christ for Life Today"	Sermons from the Old Testament "Finding God in Bible History"	Popular Doctrinal Sermons "What Christians Believe"	Mediterranean Geography "Bible Landmarks in Today's Headlines"
Christmas to Easter — *Recruiting*	"The Kingdom of Heaven"	Gospel Sermons from the Life of Christ	Evangelistic Sermons "What It Means to Be a Christian"	Bible Readings About Personal Work Selected Passages
Easter to Pentecost — *Instructing*	"Great Chapters in the Bible"	Gospel Sermons About the Days After Easter	"The Ten Commandments" or "The Heroes of the Church"	Bible Readings Missions and Trusteeship
Pentecost to September — *Heartening*	"Early Kings and Prophets"	Messages of Hope and Cheer Life-Situation Sermons	Outdoor Services (?) "Parables in St. Matthew"	Bible Songs Favorite Psalms and Hymns

other times of the week than on Sunday mornings. In an exceptional community such proposals may not prove feasible, but under fairly normal conditions a spirit of contagious enthusiasm on the part of the minister should arouse a corresponding feeling among the officers and members, as well as others out in the community. At any rate, there is today a widespread need for the kind of pastoral teaching that one can best give at hours of social worship other than Sunday morning.

Instead of thinking further about the program, let us now look at the diagram opposite. This bird's-eye view shows how the writer would plan for a given congregation in a particular year. Any mature pastor who studies the work sheet will discover ways in which he can formulate a program better adapted to the needs of his parish during the next twelve months. If he already has a plan, which may not yet be down on paper, he can use this one to check up on his ways of working.

One reason for showing the work sheet now is to prepare for the coming chapters. There is also a desire to encourage the young pastor in drawing up a program for the ensuing year's pulpit work. If he is new in the practical affairs of the ministry, he may be overlooking some of the vitamins that are essential for the healthy soul.

In any case, the only person, under God, who can tell what the local church needs from the pulpit during the coming year is the pastor. Under the guidance of the Holy Spirit the minister should be able to plan his pulpit work with practical wisdom, and then he should carry out his program with increasing joy. God bless him and make him a means of blessing, more and more!

Chapter II

OBSERVING SPECIAL DAYS

IN PLANNING FOR THE YEAR ONE BEGINS WITH THE SPECIAL OCCA-
sions. In every local church a number of red-letter days ought
to stand out on the calendar. The reference here is to the services
in the sanctuary, especially the sermon. The technical name for
any such message is the "occasional sermon." The character of
the special day guides in the choice of the text, in the wording
of the topic, and in the planning of the introduction. Thus each
such day should have a distinctive message, with a tone color
all its own.

Planning for the pulpit work on special occasions affords a
test of a minister's piety, brains, and resourcefulness. So does
the carrying out of the program for any one of them. A man's
usefulness as a preacher depends a good deal on his ability to
represent God aright when there is something special. The reference here is not to old-fashioned oratorical flights, but to what
Raymond I. Lindquist, of Orange, New Jersey, styles "making
the momentary seem momentous."

Theoretically, a man should be at his best whenever he enters
the pulpit. Actually, every minister falls short at times. It is
doubly unfortunate if the lapse into mediocrity occurs on a red-
letter day, when the sanctuary is likely to be thronged. In order
to prevent any such debacle, why not begin to make ready a
while in advance? The preparation for any occasional sermon
brings to light more materials than one can use at the time.
Hence it is easy to start work on another message of the same
kind before the glow wrought by the special day has begun to

32

fade from the heart. Then there will be twelve months for the sermon to mature, and the silent growth will come largely through "subconscious incubation."

Sometimes it does no⁺ seem feasible to signalize a certain holiday with a special sermon. If so, the spirit of the occasion may color the earlier parts of morning worship. For instance, if Sunday falls near the Armistice Day, some of the music may be in accord with the spirit that is filling the hearts of more than a few. In a congregation where the pastor did not preach about Mother's Day the organist was complaining that the only "appropriate song" she could find was "O mother dear, Jerusalem." The minister could have done better with "Love divine, all loves excelling," and in the pastoral prayer he could have given thanks for mother love.

The choice of special days to be signalized by sermons ought to receive more attention than it does in most Protestant churches. Each parish is likely to have its own individual calendar of annual occasions, which remains much the same from year to year. If the pastor is wise, he makes his plans in accordance with the best traditions and ideals of the parish. On the other hand, he should also keep in mind the principal festivals of the historic Church Year.

THE CHRISTIAN YEAR

At present there is increasing emphasis on the Christian Year. As here employed, the term relates to a homemade program for the pulpit work. All the while there is no disposition to find fault with the Church Year. As here employed, this latter term relates to a succession of holy days whose observance is required —though even in the bodies that prescribe readings and prayers for public worship, the clergyman is largely free to determine what he shall preach. The Episcopalian[1] or Lutheran[2] minister may well base a good deal of his pulpit work directly on the appointed lessons.

The historic Church Year has holy days more or less like those that adorned the Hebrew Year, which was both religious and prescribed. In the discussion that follows, however, the emphasis is on a program drawn up in the pastor's study. He should give constant heed to the Church Year,[3] but he is even more intent on meeting the needs of his own congregation at the present time.

The Christian Year gives the place of pre-eminence to special events that have to do with the Lord Jesus Christ, for there can never be too much spiritual emphasis on such festal days as Christmas, Easter, and Pentecost. To them the Roman Church has added a host of saints' days, but of course the Protestant minister will not feel bound to prepare special sermons about all the saints. He will seek rather to glorify Christ.

Unfortunately, however, some of us have substituted for the saints' days a number of special occasions that are humanitarian and patriotic. While the causes may be worthy, certain ones are not distinctly Christian, or even religious. If some of us had gone on as we were headed for a while, notably after World War I, we might have begun by setting apart a special day in the spring for the relief of superannuated pussy cats. In these latter times, thank God, most of us have ceased putting the main emphasis on the by-products of Christianity. At last we have learned that people who love the Lord aright will take good care of His

[1] See B. S. Easton and C. H. Robbins, *The Eternal Word in the Modern World,* Scribner, 1937.

[2] See P. Z. Stronach, ed., *The Parable of the Empty Soul and Other Lenten Sermons,* Board of Publication, United Lutheran Church, 1941.

[3] See P. Brooks, *Sermons for the Principal Festivals and Fasts of the Church Year,* Dutton, 1910; C. G. Chappell, *Special Day Sermons,* Abingdon-Cokesbury, 1938.

34

dumb creatures, and that humanitarian causes depend on those who put first the love of God.

The calendar of the local church may likewise call for special sermons on occasions that are not directly Biblical.[4] Among them may be Labor Sunday, Thanksgiving, Mother's Day, and Children's Day. The sanction may be that of national custom as well as parish tradition. When there is a question about the observance of such a day, the minister should keep an open mind. If it seems best to the lay officers that he signalize the occasion with a special sermon, of course he ought to do so, and with alacrity. At the same time he should beware of what Harnack, the historian of the Church, called "the acute secularization of the Christian religion."

SPECIAL DAYS IN THE AUTUMN

The first occasional sermon may be on the Sunday immediately before Labor Day. In many a community the pastor feels that there is need of such a message from the written Word of God. In almost every city congregation now there is a lack of Spirit-filled workingmen and overseers. In the old-time village church there used to be a number of religiously-minded craftsmen, such as Adam Bede and his brother Seth in the tale by George Eliot. Like their Master, those stalwart men strove to glorify God as carpenters and builders. According to the Book, the workman who does the will of God with two brown hands is serving Him as truly as though he stood in the pulpit or at the altar.

In preaching on Labor Sunday there is a temptation to ignore God and discuss economics. Hence it is wise to start with a strong text, such as the one about the men who led in building

---

[4] See Ozora S. Davis, *Preaching on Church and Community Occasions*, University of Chicago Press, 1928.

the Tabernacle.[5]   At a time when there has been a shortage of skilled mechanics, and a tendency to exalt the white-collar job, it is good to stress what the Bible says about Bezalel and Oholiab. Because they were filled with the Spirit of God, those two men became expert artificers, and taught others to excel in the manual arts.

In preparing this message one ought to read the first series of Yale Lectures by former Dean Charles R. Brown, *The Social Message of the Modern Pulpit*.[6]   His thesis is that the Book of Exodus starts with a labor problem and that the minister should use the book as the basis of expository sermons about such conditions today.   Without accepting his interpretation as a whole, and without taking sides with Labor against Capital, or vice versa, any minister can find in Dean Brown's book the seed-thoughts for a number of helpful sermons.

Is it not time that ministers begin to rediscover the soul of the friend who toils with his hands?   Recently our home church completed the erection of additional rooms for the Bible school, as well as new arrangements for social gatherings.   The first meal in the new quarters was served by the officers of the congregation in honor of the men who had done the manual labor, as well as the contractor and the architect.   In the procession at the dedicatory exercises these same workingmen occupied positions of honor.   Even the Roman Catholics among them must have felt that some Protestants love the Church of God and the souls of workingmen.

Somehow the Church ought to proclaim the dignity of labor. Human beings have gifts differing according to their ministry. We who serve God in other ways should rejoice in the achievements of the men who supply us with bread and of those who

[5] Exod. 35:30-31; cf. Exod. 20:9; Matt. 25:20-21; John 5:17; et al.
[6] Scribner, 1912.

erect our homes. Likewise should the nation order its affairs so that there will be honorable work and a living wage for every man who desires to use his God-given powers in the service of other people. The topic of such a special sermon may be "The Spirit of God's Workmen," or else "The Gospel of Labor."

This is the gospel of labour, ring it, ye bells of the kirk!
The Lord of Love came down from above, to live with the men who
    work.[7]

In a rural community there may be no call for a special sermon on Labor Sunday. But at eleven o'clock on a Lord's Day in September there is a beautiful opportunity to signalize the opening of the public schools on the following day. Except for the home and the church, no institution affects the work of the Kingdom so much as the public schools. If the regular pulpit work during the fall is to be from Exodus, the special sermon may be about the education of the boy Moses.[8] The topic may be "How God Raises Up a Leader," or else "What the Bible Says About School."

The emphasis should be religious. The sermon may deal with the sort of spiritual nurture that begins at birth in a godly home, continues for years in the right sort of school, and reaches its height in the world of affairs. Most important of all, as the guiding and controlling power, is Almighty God. He enabled Moses to take advantage of all the culture in Egypt, the most progressive nation then on earth. In these latter times He must be raising up more than one strong deliverer who will someday set the people free from oppression.

[7] "The Toiling of Felix," from *The Poems of Henry van Dyke*, Scribner, 1920, p. 100.
   [8] Acts 7:22.

As for the Sunday preceding Armistice Day, perhaps there need be no special sermon. During the past few decades world history has been so kaleidoscopic that it is difficult to set up an enduring holiday that has to do with war, and it may prove even harder to keep the pulpit work on such an occasion from becoming secular. In any one year, as a rule, a single sermon of the sort may be sufficient, and the best time for that one may be on the Sunday prior to Thanksgiving Day.

The reason for stressing Thanksgiving, or the Sunday preceding, is that the day calls for a message about God. If the state of the times leads the hearers to expect a deliverance about war, a sermon by Phillips Brooks may prove suggestive. During the period from 1859 to 1869, when he was a rector in Philadelphia, by the grace of God he kept his heart free from bitterness and bloodthirstiness. After the strife was over he could preach about "Egyptians Dead Upon the Seashore." [9] The dominant theme was that the remembrance of a past triumph through faith should bring courage and strength for the struggle of life today. Is there no need for such a message now?

At Thanksgiving time the pastor may choose his text from the song of Moses and the people after their deliverance at the Red Sea.[10] The Lord is the Defender in whom we trust amid days of peril, the Deliverer through whom we escape from every foe, and the God for whom we build the home church as a memorial of redeeming grace. Such were the sentiments of the Hebrew people at their best, but the song of thanksgiving welled up from a single heart. So is it the province of the man in the pulpit now to voice the unspoken aspirations of many hearts.

The Thanksgiving season is a good time to preach about religion in terms of deliverance, for that is the dominant theme

[9] Exod. 14:30*b;* see *The Battle of Life,* Dutton, 1910; pp. 55-70.
[10] Exod. 15:2.

38

of Exodus. In the entire history of the Hebrews no other event brought forth so many expressions of gratitude, and so many exhortations to service, as the deliverance from bondage. Throughout the New Testament sounds forth the same note, for Christianity is the religion of redemption. The word "redemption" means deliverance through payment of a ransom, for our freedom from sin came through the death of the Redeemer. That is our supreme reason for gratitude.

Today, as perhaps never before, we should give thanks for our nation: God has not so blessed any other people. In 1620 He watched over the Pilgrim Fathers at Plymouth, and in 1621 He led them to set apart a day in November for thanksgiving because of "bountiful" harvests. Among all the year's festivals, this one is most distinctly Protestant. Thus it enables us as a nation to recall our noblest traditions and renew our loftiest ideals.

Unfortunately, Thanksgiving Day has become largely secular and commercial. Hence it may be wise to hold the services on the Sunday preceding, but scarcely on the one following. Throughout the Christian Year, especially during the period before Christmas, the home church should encourage the people of God to look forward. Seldom is it wise to preach a special sermon about a day that has gone by. "Lead on, O King Eternal!"

The Thanksgiving message may have to do with our reasons for gratitude as a nation, as a local church, or as individuals. Rarely is it wise to compress all of this into a single omnibus discourse. Unless the speaker is skillful, the effect is like that of shooting a blunderbuss, which aims at everything and hits nothing. Once or twice in a lifetime, perhaps when bidding farewell to the active ministry, a parish clergyman can try to speak as a statesman in the Kingdom of God, but as a rule the sermon by the pastor should be specific. Whenever he preaches, his motto should be, "This one thing I do."

Listen to John Henry Newman, who excelled as a pastoral teacher:

Definiteness is the life of preaching. . . . . Nothing is so fatal to the effect of the sermon as the habit of preaching on two or three subjects at once. . . . . No one can carry away much from a discourse on the general subject of virtue. . . . . He [the preacher] must aim at imprinting on the heart what will never leave it, and this he cannot do unless he employs himself on some definite object.[11]

As an example of specific pulpit work, though not from Exodus, think of a Thanksgiving sermon in a year when every heart is heavy because of war. The text is about King David,[12] who is on the field of battle, while across the way are the hosts of the Philistines. Suddenly, moved by homesickness, the king cries out: "Oh that one would give me drink of the water of the well of Bethlehem, which is by the gate!" At once three of his mightiest warriors steal away and at peril of their lives bring him a draught of water from the old home well. He does not put a drop to his lips, but pours the water on the ground.

In terms of today, here is a sacrament of friendship, a proof of loyalty, and an oblation to God. Thus we have an object lesson showing the beauty of sentiment, the glory of manliness, and the wonder of sacrifice. What a message for Thanksgiving, or any other festival time when God's children should be thinking of religion and life in terms of loyalty and sacrifice! On such a day the voice from the pulpit should inspire Christian people to set up standards that will help them live and die with courage and hope.

[11] *The Idea of a University,* Longmans, Green, London, 1891, p. 411.
[12] II Sam. 23:15.

THE CHRISTMAS SEASON

Still more directly Christian should be the sermons during December. Starting early in the fall the pulpit work should lead up gradually to the message of the Incarnation. After Thanksgiving there may be a morning sermon or two from a prophetic book. The choice of the prophecy should depend in part on what one plans to do later. If the messages between Christmas and Easter are to be from St. Luke, one can prepare for them by preaching from the Book of Micah.

The prediction about the birth of the Messiah at Bethlehem[13] may lead to a message about "The Glory of God in Our Village." If one is preaching from a city pulpit the topic may be "Good News for Common People." If the sermons for the next quarter are to be from St. Matthew, one can prepare the way by preaching from Isaiah, who more than any other prophet wrote about the Messianic King. Hence the subject of the discourse may be "The Ideal Ruler for Today";[14] but a better topic, because more spiritual, would be "The Crown Rights of the Redeemer."

On the second Sunday before Christmas the sermon from St. Matthew may be about "The Heart of the Christmas Gospel."[15] The central idea here is deliverance from sin. A week later the topic may be "The Inner Meaning of Christmas."[16] When the hearts of men and women are filled with doubts and fears, the call is to worship God as He makes Himself known through the Incarnate Christ. The motive that brought the Saviour from heaven to earth, and led Him at last to the Cross, was love for

[13] Mic. 5:2; cf. 5:5*a*.
[14] Isa. 9:6-7.
[15] Matt. 1:21.
[16] Matt. 1:23.

God and men. To be a Christian now means to share His longing for the redemption of the world.

According to the plan in view, however, the messages leading up to Easter Day are to be from St. Luke, for no other Gospel is so rich in materials about Christmas. Only the Third records "The Songs at Our Saviour's Birth," which are the Magnificat, the Benedictus, the Gloria in Excelsis, and the Nunc Dimittis.[17] These Latin titles from the Vulgate need to be interpreted in the pulpit. This is especially true in the Protestant Episcopal Church, where the four songs bulk large in the majestic liturgy.

Any one of them will provide materials for a moving sermon. The closing words of the Benedictus,[18] for instance, could be the starting point of a message about "The Christmas Gospel of Light." The Gloria in Excelsis may lead to a sermon for the Sunday before Christmas. If so, the topic may be "The Yuletide Message of Peace." When the larger part of the "civilized" world has been at war, and the skies everywhere are black with forebodings, the promise of a world without war may seem like "the baseless fabric of a dream." Nevertheless, the song of the angels affords our war-weary world its only hope, for "this man shall be our peace." [19] Especially at Christmas time the minister of the Gospel should be the messenger of good will among men, for that is the spirit of the Incarnation and of the Yuletide.

On the Sunday after Christmas the sermon may be connected with New Year's Day, for the season fits in admirably with the plan to preach from St. Luke. The businessman is taking his inventory and making ready for the next twelve months. He

[17] Luke 1:46-55; 1:68-79; 2:14; 2:29-32.
[18] Luke 1:78-79.
[19] Mic. 5:5a.

42

should be attracted by a message about the beginning of the Master's life among men, and the need for making a new start in religion. The text may be from the lips of John the Baptist, a mighty soul-winning preacher.

The summons is to get right with God, here and now: "Bring forth therefore fruits worthy of repentance." [20] The word translated "repentance" means a turning to God, an about-face. Thus the minister can sound the keynote for the coming quarter; that is soul winning. "Prepare ye the way of the Lord." Such religion leads to many sorts of service, but back of them all is personal acceptance of Christ as Saviour and Lord. Why not determine now to make the next New Year's sermon evangelistic?

SPECIAL DAYS IN THE SPRING

There need be no other "occasional" message before Palm Sunday. Meanwhile the winter months afford a wealth of illustrative materials, to be drawn largely from the lives of our national heroes. While the plan in mind calls for preaching about the Saviour, there may be illustrative examples from the biographies of Lincoln and Washington, or Lee and Jackson. If the minister is able to use concrete facts from such a source in a sermon about the kindness of the Lord Jesus, or the need for the Church in days of war, the teacher of history in the high school will be glad that her pastor keeps to his own field, and that he knows how to use secular biography for the glory of God.

The week beginning with Palm Sunday may call for a series of special sermons, a subject to which we shall later return. What concerns us now is that all the messages during Holy Week ought to enforce the truths that the minister has been stressing ever since Christmas. Especially should the sermons on

[20] Luke 3:8*a;* or 3:4.

Palm Sunday, Good Friday, and Easter be of the highest order, both intellectually and spiritually. They are more certain to be so if the pastor keeps them in mind throughout the preceding months and determines by God's grace to be at his best on the crowning days of the Christian Year.

Almost equally rich in preaching values is Pentecost. Hitherto the day has seldom received due recognition, but now it is coming into its own. After Easter everything in the pulpit should prepare the way for Pentecost. The intervening messages may be about the Living Christ, or the Christian Church. On Pentecost itself, however, the sermon will surely have to do with the Holy Spirit, as He alone is the Power of God for winning the world to Christ.

In the late spring and early summer there may be only two special sermons: on Mother's Day and on Children's Day. Once in a while local conditions call for preaching about Memorial Day, the close of the public schools, or the Fourth of July. Since all five occasions are modern and American, the emphasis is likely to be on the human, not the divine. Since the period between Pentecost and the August vacation averages only about ten weeks, it would not be expedient to set apart five special days, all of which are semisecular. With such a preaching program the sanctuary might seem like a Rotary or Kiwanis Club.

Any one of these days tests a man's spirituality, as well as his courage. In the special address is he able to bring out the religious values of what appears to be secular? Can he preach so as to exalt the Lord Jesus? On Mother's Day, especially, can the minister be human without seeming sentimental? One way to avoid some of the pitfalls is to take the special sermon from the field where he is preaching regularly. If the date for Mother's Day coincides with Pentecost, as sometimes happens, the morning sermon may deal with Pentecost, and the evening message with Mother's Day, or vice versa. A more delicate undertaking is to blend the two ideas in a single sermon, of which the topic may be "The Church in a Mother's Home." [21] The Biblical setting is the Upper Room, which seems to have been where the disciples assembled to receive the Holy Spirit. There is a good deal of ground for believing that the Upper Room was in the home of Mary, the mother of John Mark.[22] If so, the Christian Church was born in the house of a godly woman. Especially in a sanctuary where the people worship directly over the place set apart for the church school, it is good to preach about the Upper Room.

On Children's Day the special sermon may be in keeping with what the pastor is doing throughout June and July. If he is preaching from selected psalms he can find in this same field all sorts of messages for boys and girls, or their fathers and mothers. If on other Sunday mornings the minister has a junior sermon, on Children's Day he should address adults, and the message to them should be about the little ones. Such a sermon is of interest to some men and women who have no children of their own to love. But if on other Sundays there is no message for boys and girls, on Children's Day the preaching may be to them directly.

It is difficult to hold the attention of boys and girls throughout a full-length sermon, even if one thinks in terms of fifteen minutes, with twenty as the upper limit. On the contrary, it is possible to overdo this modern business of being brief. In a congregation that stresses preaching it would not be wise to substitute a seven-minute "pep talk" for a full-fledged message from God. As for other exercises customary in Children's Day pro-

[21] Acts 1:14; cf. 1:13a.
[22] See J. A. Robertson, *The Hidden Romance of the New Testament*, Doran. n.d., pp. 25-42.

grams, such performances are more in keeping with the informality of the church school rooms than with the spirit of God's sanctuary.

In preaching to boys and girls it is good to have a striking text, especially if it is short. The way of presenting it should be vivid, but not exciting. A well-known line of thought comes from the passage: "Thy word have I hid in mine heart, that I might not sin against thee." [23] The subject may be "The Bible in a Boy's Heart," and the treatment may be textual. If so, conventionally it runs as follows: "The best Book"—"in the best place"—"for the best purpose." Ordinarily this is enough for the young hearer to carry home and remember. If the minister is skillful in the use of repetition, he can likewise show that a good place for the Book is in the hand, a better place is in the head, and the best place is in the heart. Whatever the main ideas, they need to sound forth again and again, like the recurring motifs in a fugue melody. If the customs of the sanctuary permit the boys and girls to take an active part in the service, at intervals they can rise to repeat with the pastor the words of his text, or anything else that he wishes them to remember forever. However, at best such co-operative preaching is difficult; and with a large group of restless boys and girls it would be too risky, for the situation might get out of hand.

The minister who loves the boys and girls is able to present his chosen truth so clearly and attractively that each of them will see and remember. Instead of attempting to say many things, he utters only a few, for well does he know the value of "precept upon precept; line upon line, ... here a little, and there a little." [24] From his mother at her knee he may have learned the wisdom of meaningful repetition.

[23] Ps. 119:11.
[24] Isa. 28:10.

According to a familiar legend, a friend once asked Susanna Wesley why she kept telling little John the same thing twenty times. She replied that he was not quick and that if she told him only nineteen times he might forget, but that if she did it twenty he would remember as long as he lived. Her method seems to have been successful, for in later years her son did remember. Well he knew his mother's Bible; better still, he loved his mother's Saviour; best of all, he proclaimed his mother's Gospel.

It is easier to hold attention by breaking up a sermon into a few sections. One way of doing so is to choose as a theme song a familiar hymn. Early in the hour one has the boys and girls sing the words as their junior anthem. In the sermon, after five or six minutes one has the people rise to sing with the boys and girls a part of the theme song. Beyond the middle of the sermon one has them do the same thing, and again near the close. Thus the refrain should keep echoing in every heart for days and years to come.

On a Sunday morning before Christmas the writer once spoke to boys and girls about "The Christmas Candle." He started with the old legend: "On Christmas Eve if you put in the window of your home a lighted candle, the Child of Bethlehem will come in to bless you every one." The theme song that morning was "Thou didst leave Thy throne and Thy kingly crown," set to the familiar tune, "Margaret." The emphasis was on the refrain,

> O come to my heart, Lord Jesus,
> There is room in my heart for Thee.

After the first stage in the sermon everyone stood to sing, "O come to my heart, Lord Jesus"; after the second, "O come to my home"; after the third, "O come to our church." In

47

preparing the message there was a temptation to keep on with still other variations, such as "O come to our school," and "O come to our world"; but it seemed wiser to stop with something simple and then leave the rest to the imagination.

Some other day, after the boys and girls have become accustomed to team play with their friend in the pulpit, he can deal with the text, "As cold waters to a thirsty soul, so is good news from a far country." [25] The theme song may be "O Zion, haste, thy mission high fulfilling." If so, the minister has the congregation sing each time a different stanza, with the uniform refrain. The subject may be "Good News for a Bad World": the Gospel is Good News for people up North, over in the East, out in the West, and down in the South. Thus there is an acrostic based on the word NEWS. In a blackboard talk one could use these letters to mark the four parts of the Cross, but why not simply appeal to the imagination?

We have now considered some of the occasions that call for special sermons. Strive as a man will to keep the number down, the calendar is almost certain to include nine or ten red-letter days. The writer recommends the lower number. Ideally, these special occasions should be distributed over the year, so as to have a breathing space between every two. But Christmas and New Year's, as well as Palm Sunday and Easter, must always come close together. Even so, nine or ten red-letter days should lend variety to the year's pulpit work.

Four of these occasions are distinctly Christian; for Christmas, Palm Sunday, Easter, and Pentecost have to do with the heart of our holy faith. The other five do not center in the Redeemer. Hence Labor Sunday—or the opening of the public schools— Thanksgiving Day, New Year's, Mother's Day, and Children's Day seem to be human rather than divine. Nevertheless, for

[25] **Prov. 25:25.**

any of these occasions it is possible to prepare a message that will be full of Gospel marrow.

Such a celebration ought to be unique. It should have a glow all its own, and there may even be a touch of splendor. If the minister wears a pulpit gown he may also put on his colored hood. The sermon should appeal to the eye as well as the ear, and move the will to action. In order to prepare aright, the speaker should begin a good while before and enter into the spirit of the occasion imaginatively. If he does so, the message will linger in the hearer's mind as long as he lives, and especially will it keep shining in the soul of the growing boy.

How can one determine whether or not to celebrate a certain day? In each case a deciding factor may be the program for that season of the year. During the fall one is striving to reveal the will of God as it concerns the man in the pew. Between Christmas and Easter one is bringing the hearer face to face with the Lord Jesus, and after Easter one is exalting the Living Christ. With such a spiritual program one dare not turn aside for anything secondary. To such a suggestion the reply may be: "I am doing a great work, so that I cannot come down: why should the work cease, whilst I leave it, and come down to you?"[26]

Ideally, every special sermon ought to stand out with a splendor all its own. It should rise above the messages of other days much as the Matterhorn towers above the surrounding peaks, for it is "unmatched in all the world." The glory, however, ought to be unto the name of God, for no special sermon, or any other, should call attention to the preacher and away from his Lord.

In view of all these facts, the minister should thank God for the preaching values in the Christian Year. Instead of trying to run a homiletical merry-go-round, which would have motion

[26] Neh. 6:3.

without progress, he can lead his friends stage by stage into the mountain country of God. Instead of using any red-letter day for some spectacular stunt, he can make the hour of worship one of life's memorable experiences, and the sermon a mountaintop vision of Christ. If so, why should the pastor of a large church in a nearby city insist on celebrating Easter morning by having in the sanctuary a bevy of canary birds?

At this point we may pause, so that each of us may think about the special days that are to stand out on his church calendar during the coming twelve months. Then let each resolve: "By the grace of God every one of those messages shall shine like a star in the sky. Each star shall differ from every other, and all together shall shine for the glory of God."

UNDERGIRDING

From September to Christmas

Chapter III

FINDING GOD IN BIBLE HISTORY

SOON AFTER THE SUMMER VACATION THE MORNING SERMONS
should begin leading up towards Christmas. In order to make
clear the background of the Christian religion the minister can
preach from Old Testament history. Let us assume that during
the previous year the morning sermons in autumn have been
from Genesis, which is about "God in the Home." The first
book of the Bible is an unfailing source of materials for the pulpit
today, and the same is true of Exodus, from which one can
preach during the coming fall.

Here we move in a different world, for between Genesis and
Exodus there is a gap of several generations. The single
patriarchal household has multiplied into thirteen tribes. Usually
we think of them as twelve, but if we include Levi, to which
Moses and Aaron belonged, we have thirteen. This number
makes us think of our own early history, with the thirteen col-
onies. Far more than in our colonial times, the people of God
in Egypt were enduring affliction. As in a volume of early
American history,[1] in Exodus we can watch the transformation
of thirteen units, widely divergent, into the beginnings of national unity. In the Book of Exodus, then, we learn about "The
God of the Nation."

Such use of Biblical history in the pulpit should lead both

---

[1] See A. B. Hart, *The Formation of the Union*, Longmans, Green, 1925; cf.
Sherwood Eddy, *The Kingdom of God and the American Dream*, Harper, 1941,
ch. iii, "Colonial America"; W. W. Sweet, *Religion in Colonial America*, Scribner,
1942.

pastor and people to become acquainted with a major book in the Bible, and to become concerned about the blessing of God on the Mediterranean world today. Now that the eyes of thoughtful men have been fixed on Egypt and the Red Sea, it is good to recall how in the days of old the Lord God watched over His people there. All the while we should remember His lovingkindness to us as a people, especially in the days of our early history.

GOD AND THE NATION

In preparing for sermons about the nation the minister may need to spend several months with the Book of Exodus. He should be familiar with the geography and history of Egypt, and have constantly at hand a commentary or two.[2] Most of all should he study the Book of Exodus, part by part. Then each discourse will stand over against the background of the book as a whole.

These preliminary studies will probably require an hour or two a day for two or three months. In mastering a book of the Bible from which one is later to preach, a safe rule is to let the period of study be as long as the time to be covered by the course of sermons. Just as in a fruit tree the roots underground may be as extensive as the branches athwart the sky, so in our work the quantity of the fruit depends largely on the extent of the roots.

The Book of Exodus is well worth knowing, for it deals with the early days of the people who founded the Hebrew Church, wrote the Old Testament, as well as nearly all the New, and gave to the world the Lord Jesus. But even if Exodus were little more than the setting of the Ten Commandments, the

[2] See J. H. Breasted, *A History of Egypt,* Scribner, 1912; A. H. McNeile, *The Book of Exodus,* Westminster Commentaries, 1908; S. R. Driver, *Exodus,* Cambridge Bible, 1911.

modern man should be familiar with the background of that massive Law.

On the human level the action in Exodus centers around Moses, who was perhaps the mightiest man of Old Testament times. In reading Bible history, as well as any other part of the Scriptures, it is good to stress the human leader, but only as the agent of Almighty God. In Exodus the emphasis is not so much on Moses and the Children of Israel as on the Lord God of Hosts and His redemptive purpose.

Among all the sermons from Exodus, the introductory one may be the most difficult to prepare, yet it should be the most vital. In it the pastor may give a bird's-eye view of Exodus. The purpose is to guide the layman in reading the book at home and in hearing about it from the pulpit. In order to quicken the desire for such reading at home, the bulletin for a number of weeks may announce that the morning sermons until after Thanksgiving will be from Exodus, and that the people can help the minister by reading in their homes the entire book, especially the first twenty chapters.

The topic of the opening sermon may be "How God Watches Over the Nation." [3] The minister can ask the people to look at Exodus from five points of view. The first few chapters deal with the birth of the national leader. The next part has to do with the desire of the people for liberty. Then the book describes their departure from the land of bondage. The central chapters are about the giving of the Law. The latter part of Exodus concerns a common center, which is religious, and corresponds with the church on the green in the heart of a New England village.

In such a summary the facts seem tame, but in the sermon the movement should be dramatic, for in Exodus the action

[3] The text may be the keynote of the book, Exod. 20:2.

is often thrilling. If a novelist or playwright, such as Thomas Mann or James M. Barrie, were mulling over these facts before he presented them in five successive scenes, he might begin with the human problem as it concerns the mother and her newborn babe. After he aroused concern for God's suffering poor, the artist might make clear how God set His people free and then molded them into a nation.

Especially is the first half of Exodus full of stirring action, almost as much so as the latter part of Genesis. After Thomas Mann has completed his current series of novels about Joseph, perhaps the next character in line will be Moses. He is a massive personality, as anyone can see at Rome in Michelangelo's statue "Moses." A historical study of this gigantic figure would begin with the mastery of Exodus, which is the lengthened shadow of the mighty leader. The shadow is cast by light that comes from the throne of God.

In preaching about an entire book of the Bible a man needs to be an artist who knows how to paint with a large brush. Otherwise he may become bewildered by details, or else busy himself with showing the skeleton of the book. Pulpit work that merely relates facts, or else outlines a book of the Bible, is likely to be worth no more than it costs, which may be next to nothing. Preaching is the interpretation of living truth, and that calls for the use of the imagination. Whatever the form of the sermon, it should sound forth the keynote of Exodus, which is the will of God for the nation.

In this sort of synthetic study the writer once had a unique experience. Immediately after the first World War he was thinking much about the smaller countries of Europe. He kept asking himself, "What will be necessary if Poland, Czechoslovakia, or any other assemblage of diverse peoples, is to become a united nation?" He concluded that the essentials for statehood are five:

a leader such as George Washington; a desire for separate existence; an effective break for freedom; a body of laws; and, above all, some sort of religious fervor. After the list was complete, the compiler felt the glow that comes occasionally through "creative endeavor." Then, to his chagrin, he found that he had merely reproduced the basic framework of Exodus. So much for a man's "original thinking"! Whenever it is worthy, all of it comes from God, and most of it through the Scriptures.

Today we are wondering whether or not certain small peoples across the Atlantic will survive. Only the Lord can tell, but we hope that in Europe there will be some kind of federal union, with a large measure of local autonomy. Here in the United States we have long been accustomed to the benefits that accrue from having bound together in one nation diverse geographical units. If all this appears to smack of politics, rather than religion, the fault is with the form of statement, for the principles themselves come from the heart of God's Holy Book.

GOD AND THE LEADER

The next subject may be "How God Raises Up a Leader." [4] While there is a world of difference between the two men, there is an interesting parallel between the experience of Moses and that of George Washington. Each of them in his different fashion was to guide thirteen individualistic groups in their struggles for liberty. Before embarking on the enterprise, each of those men as the commander needed to know the people that he was to guide, the forces that he was to oppose, and the God that he was to represent.

In such pulpit work the emphasis may be on the Providence of God as He takes care of a single babe. In the Hebrew home where Moses was born he shared the hardships and perils of that

[4] Heb. 11:27b.

oppressed people. A little later in the household of Pharaoh's daughter the lad came to know the inner life of the ruling classes in Egypt. Best of all, out in the wilderness of Sinai the future leader came to know Almighty God as the Lord of his life and the Redeemer of the people. All these facts are stranger than fiction.

Still more gripping should be the message "How God Watches Over the Child." [5] Most moving are the records about the perils of childbirth and motherhood under ancient totalitarian despotism. For a parallel with this part of Exodus, read about Herod's slaughter of the innocent babes at Bethlehem.[6] Then turn again to Exodus and note how the Lord makes use of the mother and the midwives, the sister and the king's daughter, in keeping alive one tiny babe, "with no language but a cry."

Even more vital should be the sermon, "How God Makes Himself Known." [7] Today, as of old, the Lord reveals Himself to each person in a different fashion. Seldom is the revelation so thoroughly unique as with Moses at the burning bush. There is only one record of a bush that burned without being consumed. But the truth that shone out before Moses at that far-off moment is one that concerns us all today: Amid the fiercest persecutions and trials the Church of the Living God is sure to survive. *"Nec tamen consumebatur."*

In a day when the Christian Church across the seas appears to have its back against the wall, it is good to assure God's people that His Church will endure. In a time when the kings of the earth have set themselves, and the rulers have taken counsel together, in their determination to do away with the Church of Christ, it is heartening to know that He still reigns,

[5] Exod. 2:9a.
[6] Matt. 2:16-18.
[7] Exod. 3:2, or 3:5.

and that all is well with the Church when it is true to Him. This is one reason why the favorite emblem of Presbyterian bodies everywhere, especially in Scotland, is the burning bush.

The emphasis, however, should be on Almighty God, not on the burning bush that is only a symbol which appeals to the imagination. The message that shines out from the bush is the power and the perseverance of God. After Moses had learned that lesson, he went forth a changed man; at last he was ready to become the leader of God's people.

The transforming experience came to Moses in a place where he felt at home. Day after day for years he had fed his flock on that lonely mountainside. But never before had he beheld a bush aflame. Ever afterward to him that spot was holy ground.

For the man of God's choosing, the burning bush now is the place where he learns to think of the Lord as the Deliverer, and of himself as the leader. In such an experience there are always three factors, each of which is personal: God, the people, and oneself. In the hour of vision the man set apart by God for leadership resolves to put Him first, others second, and self last. This is close to the inner meaning of a religious life, for the spirit is akin to that of the Cross.

GOD AND HIS PEOPLE

The next subject may be "How God Blesses in Hard Times."[8] Like almost every other major book in the Bible, Exodus has to do with days of adversity. To those Hebrews, whose fathers had long been free, bondage in Egypt was as bitter as gall. Nevertheless, in the Providence of God, during their sojourn in an alien land those serfs became proficient in building and other manual arts. Henceforth they would not be obliged to

[8] Exod. 6:7.

dwell in tents that could be blown down. When at last they were ready to go out from Egypt they were largely equipped for existence as a separate nation.

Among those Hebrews sufferings undeserved gave birth to a determination for freedom. If they had been happy in Egypt, they might have been tempted to settle down permanently along the Nile, but that was not the will of God. Under His guidance, when the burdens of existence in Egypt became too heavy for human beings to bear, they began to yearn for a country of their own.

Thus the oppression in Egypt affords a series of object lessons in the practical workings of God's Providence. Even in the darkest experiences of life He can make all things work together for good to them that love Him. He can make even the wrath of man to praise Him.[9]

Close akin is the message, "How God Makes His People Strong." [10] If the oppression intensified the desire of the Hebrews for liberty, the ten plagues increased their determination to go out from the land of bondage. To that childlike people, most of whom could not read and write, the plagues were visible object lessons, sermons in action.

The stress, however, should be on God, not the plagues. Certain scholars,[11] who believe in Old Testament miracles, think that those portents were largely God's ways of using what we know as natural causes. If so, back of them was the hand of Almighty God. Through the plagues He led the Children of Israel to trust in the Most High, to regard themselves as His servants, and to resist the rulers of Egypt. To this very hour,

[9] Rom. 8:28; Ps. 76:10a.

[10] Exod. 11:1a, or Acts 7:36.

[11] See *International Standard Biblical Encyclopedia*, Chicago, 1930, IV, 2403; G. L. Robinson, *The Bearing of Archaeology on the Old Testament*, American Tract Society, 1941, pp. 40-44.

He alone can control the forces of earth and sky and sea; He can use them all for the good of His people. Is there no need of such a message now?

In the sermon, "How God Sets His People Free," [12] the emphasis is on the Passover. To the Hebrews, ever after the Exodus, the Passover was the supreme symbol of their deliverance from a bondage somewhat like hell. The annual feast made them think much about the fathers as crossing through the Red Sea and then as journeying toward the Promised Land. Ever with those early pilgrims, keeping watch above His own, was God, the Father Almighty.

The Passover was the symbol of redemption from bondage. That in turn was the chief event in Hebrew history. Between the creation of the world and the coming of the Messiah, nothing appealed to the imagination of the devout Hebrew so much as the deliverance from bondage. In song and story and sermon he exulted in the mercy of God, who had led His people out of Egypt.[13]

Today the Christian Church looks upon the Passover Feast as the Old Testament counterpart of the Lord's Supper. Each of the two festivals is the God-given symbol of redemption from a fate worse than death. In the Providence of God, the Crucifixion of Christ took place at the season of the Passover. From that day to this the Church has sung about redemption in terms derived from Exodus. For example, in the eighth century A.D. John of Damascus wrote two of our most beloved Easter hymns. In one we rejoice because "God hath brought His people forth into joy from sadness." In the other we sing about "the Passover of gladness, the Passover of God."

After the Lord of Hosts had delivered His people, they still

[12] Exod. 13:14.
[13] See Pss. 78:42-53; 105:24-39.

61

needed His guidance. In a sense they had to rely upon God more completely than ever before. His leading by day was through the pillar of cloud and at night through the pillar of fire.[14] On a childlike people those portents in the heavens must have made a tremendous impression. To us more sophisticated folk, who dwell beneath Western skies, a cloud is a matter of course. In fact, we seldom look up at the skies, and when we do, it is not to think about God.

In the land of the Nile at the season of the Passover a cloud in the heavens is rare. As for the pillar of fire, no one now can tell what it may have been. The spiritual meaning is what concerns us here: the cloud and the fire were God's tokens that He was with His people day and night, that He was able to protect them from the perils of the wilderness, and that He would lead them safely into the Promised Land. That is why many a believer loves to sing:

> Guide me, O Thou great Jehovah,
>   Pilgrim through this barren land;
> I am weak, but Thou art mighty;
>   Hold me with Thy powerful hand.

DOING GOD'S WILL TODAY

In such a course the pulpit work from week to week should grow more practical. The next sermon may be on the subject, "How God Leads in Days of War."[15] Like many another strong preaching text, this one embodies a striking contrast. The first part calls for waiting upon God; to Him belongeth the power, and from Him will come the victory. "Wait upon the Lord!" Here is a truth that we in the United States ought to learn,

[14] Exod. 13:21-22.
[15] Exod. 14:15; cf. 14:13-14.

for even in the sanctuary of God we sing and talk about religion and life in terms of what we can do. In a recent ecclesiastical assembly to promote world-wide missions this was the slogan at every session: "It All Depends on Me!"

Meanwhile the source of power is on high: "Be still and know that I am God." [16] Such is the spirit of His loyal followers, especially in the zero hour. Sooner or later, however, will come His call for advance. Then the Lord will say to His servant, the leader of the band whose hearts God has touched: "Wherefore criest thou unto me? speak unto the children of Israel that they go forward." This is why after a moving sermon God's people love to stand and sing "Lead On, O King Eternal."

A week later the message may be on "Teamwork for God."[17] The truth here is largely on the human level, for the passage is about what modern folk call "division of labor," or "business management," most of which is new only in name. Any such line of thought is more likely to interest and help the city executive or businessman than the farmer or housemother who cannot secure and keep a single paid helper.

The principle of teamwork also applies to the minister as an executive. The chief weakness of the average pastor as a leader of men lies in his unwillingness to delegate responsibility and then allow the other man to do the work in his own way. Perhaps unconsciously, the clergyman feels that no one else can deal with details so well as he. Like Atlas, he tries to carry the world on his shoulders, and sooner or later he breaks down beneath burdens that others would gladly have borne. Then he is tempted to blame everyone else, including God.

The reason for stressing the matter here is that if the pastor enlists the lay forces of the congregation he will have time and

[16] Ps. 46:10*a*.
[17] Exod. 18:17-26; cf. Acts 6:1-8.

energy enough for his God-given mission as student, preacher, and pastor. One Baptist minister, when called to a large parish, summoned a meeting of the official board. To those consecrated men he explained his inability to do more than one man's work, and he asked them to assume responsibility for everything except what the Lord had committed to his hands. He also secured their promise to guard him from interruptions as he engaged in morning studies. Then he gave himself wholeheartedly to what he alone could do for God. Needless to say, the work in that field has prospered. The minister has a plan which puts God first.

The ability to lead strong men as teammates grows through proper use. In *Abraham Lincoln, The War Years,* Carl Sandburg tells how in Washington the President worked with a cabinet of ill-assorted rivals, and how in the field he depended on a succession of ineffective generals. At first Lincoln knew little about the leadership of men, but gradually he inculcated in his associates the spirit of teamwork. After a while everyone in the capital city knew that the Cabinet had a leader and that the Army had a commander-in-chief.

On the human level what is the prime essential for the leadership of men in the church? Probably the ability to work with them rather than over them. The minister has to depend on volunteers, and he must know how to select the right one for each post. Publicly the choice is made by some society, but indirectly the suggestion about the proper man usually comes from the pastor, in response to a request for advice. When once the choice has been made, and duly ratified, the minister never interferes with what his teammate is doing. Whenever it is possible to do so with a clear conscience, the pastor delights to express his appreciation of such work. For a real ministerial leader and friend, church folk would gladly die.

Still more vital should be the sermon, "The Heart of the Pastor." [18] Here again the message may seem to be for the minister rather than the people, but it can do them no harm if once in a while he shows what is dearest to his heart. According to Hebrew custom, when the high priest went into the holy place he bore on his breast a plate with the names of the twelve tribes. In modern terms, the pastor carries on his heart the names of the families committed to his charge. While they are at work out in the world he should be interceding for them at the throne of grace. Such a custom is a proof that he has them on his heart, just as a mother keeps thinking and dreaming about her little ones.

More than one pastor sets apart Saturday evening as the special time to pray for the people. Family by family, and person by person, he brings his friends to the mercy seat. With a list of the names before his eyes, or better still, with the facts written on his heart, the ministering shepherd talks over with the Father God the problems and needs of every man or woman, boy or girl, in all the parish. Herein lies the source of spiritual power. If a minister prays for his people day by day, and especially on Saturday night, he can preach to them with unction on the Lord's Day.

Much more popular should be a message concerning the golden calf. The topic may be "The Sin of Blaming Somebody Else." [19] The passage suggested to Phillips Brooks his best-known discourse, "The Fire and the Calf." [20] That is said to be one of the three most famous sermons in the English tongue, the other two being "Every Man's Life a Plan of God" by Horace Bushnell and "The Reversal of Human Judgment" by James

[18] Exod. 28:29.
[19] Exod. 32:24.
[20] *Sermons Preached in English Churches*, Dutton, 1910, pp. 43-64.

B. Mozley. Two of the three texts, the two chosen by the American divines, are from the Old Testament. Viewed simply as literature, the Old Testament is more dramatic than the New.

The present-day sermon about the golden calf may stress a man's accountability for his deeds. According to the laws of God, what a person takes out of the fire depends largely upon what he has thrust in. Meanwhile, the temptation is to be like Aaron, who blamed everybody but himself. Such a practice is not fair to other people, and it causes untold injury to oneself. Most serious of all is the sin against God. Especially should the minister form the habit of accepting responsibility when his plans fail. "God be merciful to me, the sinner." [21]

The next sermon may be about "The Use of Money in Religion." [22] According to the record, the people gave to God freely of their substance. That is what they should have done with the gold which went into the making of the calf. The difference between the two events was largely one of leadership, for the people are like sheep. Under a pastor like Moses they do the will of God with their money. Under a man like Aaron they squander it in worldliness, if not in sin. Hence it seems that the pastor is largely responsible to God for how the people use their money.

Religion has much to do with the pocketbook and the bank account. When a man loves God, the church receives a liberal portion of his income. Out in the wilderness, as the Hebrews journeyed hither and thither, they learned to think of God as dwelling in the Tabernacle. That central sanctuary must have meant all the more to their hearts because into its erection had gone their silver and gold. Today, as a veteran builder of churches used to tell cautious laymen out in western Canada,

[21] Luke 18:13c, in the Greek.
[22] Exod. 36:5.

the local sanctuary gives to the work of the Kingdom "visibility and permanence."

When the cause appeals to men's hearts, they love to give. With a pastor like Moses, and with lay leaders like Bezalel and Oholiab, there should be no difficulty in securing all the money that the work of the sanctuary requires. In the scene before us the Hebrews showed their love for God by freewill offerings for His House. Erelong the treasury was full to overflowing. In modern terms, they oversubscribed the budget for current expenses. They did so with joy, and paid their pledges in cash. With such giving the Lord is well pleased, and especially with the leadership that makes it possible.

The final sermon from the Book of Exodus may be on the subject "God's People Under a Cloud." [23] Today we talk of the cloud as the symbol of an oncoming storm, just as we look on sunny skies as harbingers of mercy. So do we dread the fire, but look upon the light as a token of God's favor. In the closing chapters of Exodus, however, both the cloud and the fire are symbols of the Lord's presence in the sanctuary, and of His promise to bless those who worship Him aright.

Before we bid farewell to Exodus, we should look back on it as a whole. This book is one of the most thrilling parts of the Old Testament. Especially moving are the first twenty chapters, which culminate in God's giving the Law from Mount Sinai. Since we are to consider the Ten Commandments later, [24] we need not think about them here. Instead of using them as a part of the course from Exodus, we are to employ them as the basis for a special series.

The course from Exodus should be full of interest to the very end. In fact, the effect should be cumulative. In sermon after

[23] Exod. 40:34.
[24] See Chap. VIII, *infra*, pp. 143-55.

sermon the minister can show how God delivers His people from their adversaries, and how He guides them stage by stage in their pilgrimage towards Canaan. In every sermon the emphasis ought to be on persons rather than places, and on God rather than men. Each new message should open the eyes of the layman to behold afresh the Providence of God. When times are hard, the Lord is good.

Each of the sermons ought to be as moving as a one-act play. The essence of serious drama is in surmounting whatever obstacles lie in the pathway toward a worthy goal. Without being untrue to the facts as they are in Exodus, the minister can present them so vividly that the man in the pew will become a "seer." Gradually he should discover the will of God for our country today. Better still, the layman should determine to do God's will for himself as a lover of our fatherland.

After the course of messages about God in the nation, the churchgoer should have a new understanding of a major book in the Bible, a new love for his country as chosen of God for service among the peoples of the earth, and a new eagerness for hearing the Gospel as it will sound forth between Christmas and Easter.

Thus the Old Testament narratives prepare for the New Testament Evangel. The Book of Exodus shows how God set His children free from bondage, and then watched over their pilgrimage towards the Promised Land. The New Testament reveals how the Lord Christ has delivered us from slavery to sin, and how He is watching over us as "we nightly pitch our moving tents a day's march nearer home." What a Gospel, and what a God!

Chapter IV

PREACHING CHRISTIAN DOCTRINE

From the children's disease of being ashamed of theology, I think I have to some degree recovered. . . . . We whose profession it is to teach the inner meanings of religion find ourselves in perplexity. . . . . As ministers we ought to speak of God. We are human, however, and so cannot speak of God. We ought therefore to recognize both our obligation and our inability, and by that very recognition give God the glory. This is our perplexity. The rest of our task fades into insignificance in comparison.[1]

THESE WORDS FROM KARL BARTH HAVE HELPED TO AWAKEN CONcern about the preaching of doctrine. While many of us do not agree with him in certain other respects, we are glad for what he has done to bring Christian doctrine back into the pulpit. During the first few decades of the twentieth century the typical minister seemed to be searching for "something just as good" as old-fashioned interpretations of what Christians ought to believe, and why. But the man-made substitutes did not prove satisfactory. Today almost every thoughtful clergyman agrees with Barth that there ought to be more use of doctrine in the Christian pulpit.

Ideally, every sermon ought to be Biblical in substance, doctrinal in form, and practical in effect. The message should inspire the hearer to do the will of God, and to begin at once. This is one of the underlying assumptions in *A Preface to Chris-*

[1] *The Word of God and the Word of Man,* tr. by D. Horton, Pilgrim Press, 1928, pp. 97, 183, 186.

69

tian Theology,[2] by President John A. Mackay, who protests against the balcony view of religion. He likewise insists that Christian duty rests on a solid basis of Biblical facts.

While all of a man's preaching ought to be more or less doctrinal, there is often need for a message that is so directly. In the present chapter the meaning of the term "doctrinal sermon" is fairly broad. It is the preacher's interpretation of a vital Christian truth, for a high practical purpose. The reference is to teachings found in the Scriptures, supremely in Christ and the Cross. In short, doctrinal preaching is popular religious instruction from the pulpit.

From this practical point of view we shall look at certain facts about God, about man, and about Christ; for these are the basic truths of Christianity. We shall also consider some of the preaching values in the Apostles' Creed. Altogether we shall think about more than enough doctrinal subjects to keep a man busy on Sunday evenings throughout the fall and winter. The part of wisdom is to select what is most needful at present and to leave the remainder for another season. If anyone wishes to use the sermons on Sunday mornings, much the same principles apply.

FACTS ABOUT GOD

The chief questions that perplex the modern man have to do with God. Every problem of life and thought today leads back to a man's conception of the Most High. Especially since 1914 the young people and others in many a parish have been uncertain about God, and about everything that depends on His holy will. When they turn to father or mother, they receive little help. In school they often feel that psychology or physical science is the present-day successor to the mid-Victorian God. When

---

[2] Macmillan, 1941, chaps. ii, v. See also John S. Whale, *The Right to Believe*, Scribner, 1938; Emil Brunner, *Our Faith*, Scribner, 1936.

they come to church, they are in the mood to sing one of the old hymns "For Those at Sea." Our young folk and many others need to learn about God.

As a friend of young people the writer once had an experience that was unique. In September he was invited to tell the Hi-Y Club what he believed about God, and why. On a Tuesday evening he was to bring a mimeographed list of questions which the 250 boys were later to discuss in small groups. When the minister asked why he was to speak on such a difficult subject, the secretary replied: "In our boys' camp last month we found that these lads are more concerned about God than anything else. Sometimes their fathers and mothers tell us that their teen-age sons care for nothing save girls and games and good times. But we find that these lads are even more anxious to learn about God."

A year afterward the pastor was invited to address that Hi-Y Club on the same subject. The membership was the same, except that the seniors had gone and the freshmen were new. Twelve months later he was no longer in the community, but doubtless his successor was asked to tell the boys about God. The nature of the instruction will appear from the following questions, prepared for use in the discussion groups:

1. What does the word God suggest? Is He a Person? What kind of Person? What do you mean by God as a Person?

2. Where is God this evening? What do you think He is doing? Does He know about you personally?

3. Can you know God intimately? How can you know Him better? Is it worth while to become acquainted?

4. How is a good father like God? How is a good father not like God? What of a good mother? A good teacher?

5. Is God concerned about you individually? Does he care

71

about your school? Your games? Does He know how you spend your evenings?

6. Does belief in God help to keep you straight? Would you be different if you did not believe?

7. Would you like to live in a godless land? Would it be good for Russia to have no God?

8. Could there be more gods than one? Is it good for India to worship many gods?

9. Is God the Father of all mankind? Is He the Father of Turks? Mexicans? Japanese? Is He the Father of Mussolini? Stalin? Hitler?

10. Who is the Final Authority in such matters? How does Jesus make His answers known today? How can your church help answer these questions?

In days of war the questions would be somewhat different. Whatever the form, they should concern issues that bulk large in a man's mind as he makes ready to preach. The emphasis, however, ought to be on the answers, not the questions. Instead of trying to cover all the ground at once, the pastor should take up a single doctrine and present it concretely. A good place to start is with Divine Providence.

During the first World War a pastor in Toronto preached on "The Providence of God in the Fall of a Sparrow." [3] The emphasis was on the Christian God, not the English sparrow. The treatment was positive, not negative. Instead of trying to explain the mysteries of Providence, and justify the ways of God with men, the pastor gave a simple, clear interpretation of the truth in the text. In it the Lord Jesus tells about God's care of the sparrow, and His vastly greater concern for each of His children. The vividness of the text and the topic called for an effective

[3] Matt. 10:29-31; Robert Law, *The Grand Adventure*, McClelland and Stewart, Toronto, 1916, pp. 137-48.

opening paragraph. What could have been better than this one?

There is scarcely any truth more precious to Christian faith than that of divine Providence. It lays hold of us at every crisis of our personal history; it touches us every day and every hour; it includes in its scope our whole career from the cradle to the grave, and what lies beyond. It is indispensable to the religious interpretation of history.

Study this approach. The minister assumes that the hearer is interested. He has been alert during the reading of the Scriptures, and he has joined in the hymn immediately before the sermon. Now he is eager to learn about God's Providence. In this opening paragraph of the discourse every sentence has to do with the doctrine. Where many a preacher would devote ten minutes to a conventional analysis of the difficulties involved in accepting this truth, especially in days of war, the Canadian divine leads up to his sermon proper in sixty-three words.

The phrasing of the paragraph must have required more work than it would take to prepare for a lengthy discussion of the difficulties in believing what the Lord Jesus says about Providence. Equally careful is the wording of the proposition. It is in the second paragraph of the sermon:

Let me state briefly what that doctrine is. It is that God who made the world governs it by laws which He has ordained; not only so, but governs it for spiritual ends, for the advancement of His Kingdom, and the spiritual benefit of mankind.

Thus the minister leads up to the interpretation of his text. The emphasis, however, is on the truth, not the passage, for a doctrinal sermon is usually topical in form. The central teaching here is that the Father God watches over each of His children as carefully as though He had only one. The minister confesses that the truth "staggers" the mind. Nevertheless, he insists that it affords a lasting foundation for comfort and hope.

The dominant illustration is worthy of note. It is about the sinking of the "Titantic." A less skillful preacher would have related the incident at the start, and thus paved the way for anticlimax. But the Canadian divine first enlists the attention of his hearers. As he explains the meaning of God's Providence in terms of today there is no loss of interest. More than one woman is weeping as she thinks of her soldier son who fell the other day in a front-line trench. Everyone is asking how the minister can speak of such a person as going into the hands of God.

Toward the end of the sermon, to throw light on what he has taught, the minister relates a recent conversation with a friend. They were speaking about the "Titantic."

"I don't believe," said the layman, "that God had much if anything to do with it."

"Nevertheless," was the reply, "if you had been on board, or your wife and child, you would have wished to feel that the Lord had everything to do with it."

"I believe you're right," said the layman.

For various reasons that printed message is worthy of study. It shows how doctrinal preaching can be positive rather than negative, constructive rather than critical, and clear rather than cloudy. Above all should it be clear. Doctrine is only another name for teaching. Every vital truth ought to stand out so boldly that it will be impossible for anyone to miss the meaning. The spirit should be persuasive, so that the hearer will commit himself anew to the hands of the Father God.

There is an opening for an entire series of evening messages on "What Jesus Says about God." The texts may be from the writings of the Apostle John, which have much to do with doctrine. In the Fourth Gospel and the First Epistle there are five affirmations about God: He is Light—Life—Love—Spirit—Father.[4] Each of the five should result in a sermon full of beauty and power. For instance, when the Lord Jesus says that God is Spirit, the modern equivalent may be "Person." God is the Ideal Person, whom each of us should resemble, as His child.

The temptation is to compress all five truths into a single omnibus discourse. It would require comparatively little time to prepare, and would make practically no impression on the hearer. In the seminary classroom, where everyone is somewhat versed in theological lore, the professor would devote fifty minutes to the one subject "The Meaning of God as Love." In a congregation, where the people may not be accustomed to doctrinal preaching, twenty-five minutes is none too long for such a discourse. Popular preaching of Christian doctrine should be specific.

For instance, take "The Glory of God as Light." That was the subject of a lay sermon by a young high school teacher at Trenton, New Jersey. As a member of a teacher's training class she was to prepare a paper on some aspect of our Lord's teachings. Since she was a lover of outdoors and a student of physics, she let her imagination lead her into the mysteries of God as Light. In her paper she let everyone see that she loved the Father of lights, and that she was sorry for anyone who is groping in sin. Among students of physical science those who delve into astronomy are the most likely to be Christians. When a woman asked Henry Norris Russell, of Princeton Univeristy, a master in that field, how he as a scientist can believe in his mother's God, the reply was: "It all depends on the greatness of your God."

[4] I John 1:5; John 5:26; I John 4:8; John 4:24; 14:2.

FACTS ABOUT MAN

The call today is for preaching about God, but there is likewise need of sermons about man.[5] The high school teacher may assume that as a spiritual being man is practically nothing; the college professor may contend that in the realm of the spirit man is almost everything. Without attacking either position, the minister should teach the young folk, as well as their parents, what the Bible says about man in relation to God.

A good place to start is with the eighth psalm. It shows that in contrast with the heavens above, man is as helpless as a babe, but that in the light of our religion he is "a little lower than God." That is a height to which only the Lord Jesus has ever attained, but still it should be the ideal of every man. In the sermon the truth should be so gripping that the hearer will take it as his own. The subject of the message may be "The Glory of God in Man." [6]

Preaching about man brings the minister face to face with the fact of sin. Except at the beginning and the end of the Bible, the shadow cast by sin falls across almost every page. In the opening and the closing chapters, with their idyllic pictures of a world that is free from moral evil, there is naught save beauty. But everywhere else in the Bible the black fact of sin abounds.

In a doctrinal sermon it would be interesting to trace the psychology of sin as it lurks in the third chapter of Genesis. It would be possible, also, to present the theology of sin as it bulks large in the Epistle to the Romans. But it is easier to prepare a few case studies showing how sin works in living characters. That is how the facts appear in the Gospels, especially in St. Luke. After the minister has learned how to prepare and present a

[5] See Reinhold Niebuhr, *The Nature and Destiny of Man,* first series, Scribner, 1941.

[6] Ps. 8:4-5; cf. Heb. 2:6-7.

simple doctrinal sermon, he can try his hand on something harder.

An easy place to start is with the most wondrous of our Lord's parables. The leading character is the father. At the beginning of the tale the younger son puts himself out of right relations with his father. Like many a lad today, the young man is tempted. Because of his wrong attitude towards work and play, love and money, he falls into sin. But at last he comes to himself, and turns his face homeward, to get right with his father. "Father, I have sinned." [7]

In the parable the stress is on the father's love and forgiveness. In the far country, after he had wasted all his money, the son lived for a while in rags and filth. But then he began to long for his father. At home the son found pardon, cleansing, and peace. Like the mercy of God, that father's forgiveness was full; it was free; it was forever. If sin is man's way of putting himself out of right relations with God, forgiveness is the Father's way of restoring the son to the family circle.

Whatever the text, the sermon about sin should lead up to the truth about forgiveness. Both sin and forgiveness should stand out as facts of personal experience. Sin is no philosophical abstraction, no diabolical magnetism all about us in the air. Sin thrives only in the heart and life of a human being. There it manifests itself in countless forms; for it affects all his thoughts and feelings; it shows itself in his words and deeds. It may be positive or negative, active or passive, bold or furtive. However it appears, sin means being out of harmony with God.

A man may sin as much by his silence when he ought to speak as by his words when he ought to keep quiet. "Inasmuch as ye did it not to one of the least of these, ye did it not to me." [8] One

[7] Luke 15:21.
[8] Matt. 25:45.

night there was a heart-searching sermon from that text, under the heading, "Respectable Sins." At the church door an aged saint said to his pastor, "I see now that a man may be damned for things he never did."

Forgiveness, also, is personal. In a sermon by Harry Emerson Fosdick the subject is "Forgiveness of Sins." [9] The opening paragraphs make everyone present feel that he is a sinner. In addition to gross iniquities that make every man shudder, there are sins of temperament; sins of social injustice, most of which concern money; and sins of neglect, many of which are the worst of all. After such an account of present-day sins, the path is open for the chief message, which relates to forgiveness.

These are the climactic words: "No man's sin ever is done with until it has come through this process of forgiveness. Either your sin has been forgiven or else it is yet in you as sin. I think this is about the solemnest fact in human life."

A little later comes the closing appeal: "Go down into that secret place. Unlock that hidden door. Take out that unforgiven sin. For your soul's sake, get rid of it! But there is only one way. Whatever theology you hold, it is the way of the Cross—penitence, confession, restitution, pardon."

In short, every minister should preach about God and man, sin and forgiveness, death and judgment. This kind of pulpit work is especially appropriate during the fall, when one is laying the foundations for the year's work. Week after week the messages should prepare the way for the coming sermons about Christ. He alone is the Supreme Revealer of God and the perfect Ideal for men. The best way, therefore, to present the truth about God and man, sin and redemption, death and life everlasting, is to preach Christ.

[9] *The Secret of Victorious Living,* Harper, 1934, pp. 110-19.

FACTS ABOUT CHRIST

In preaching about the Son of God doctrinally, a good place to start is with the Fourth Gospel. In December there may be a sermon or two about the Incarnation,[10] which is the basic fact about the Lord Jesus. Supremely in Christ, beginning with His Incarnation, God makes Himself known. During the days of His flesh our Lord dwelt as in a tent,[11] and to this very hour He is our Redeemer. His purpose in coming to earth was to save us men from sin and to rule over us all. If there had been no Incarnation there could have been no Calvary and no Easter.

Sometime in January one of the sermons may be about the human nature of our Lord.[12] While the Fourth Gospel is mainly about His Deity, there is also a good deal of emphasis on His humanity. Some of us evangelical folk make the Lord Jesus seem as unreal as He is in a painting by Botticelli, but it is never so in the Gospels, where He always appears as God's idea of a Man. Christ alone is the complete Personality. At best all other human beings are only men and women in the making, whereas He is the Ideal. "Behold the Man!"

Still more vital should be the message about the Deity of Christ.[13] While in the pastorate, the writer made it a rule to preach directly on the subject once or twice every year. In a course from St. John there could be such a sermon at the beginning, to show the layman what to look for in reading the book. Then there might be another message at the end of the course, to impress on mind and heart what the Fourth Gospel tells

[10] See Charles Gore, *The Incarnation of the Son of God*, Scribner, 1900; R. L. Ottley, *The Doctrine of the Incarnation*, London, 1919; Emil Brunner, *The Mediator*, London, 1934.

[11] John 1:14, in the Greek; cf. II Cor. 8:9; Phil. 2:5-11.

[12] John 19:5b, or 4:6.

[13] John 1:1.

about Christ. In each message the aim should be to cause acceptance of Him as Saviour and Lord.

The purpose of the Fourth Gospel appears in the key verse: "These are written, that ye may believe that Jesus is the Christ, the Son of God; and that believing ye may have life in his name." [14] In a course of morning sermons from St. John the writer once closed with a message from this key verse. On that morning he witnessed a larger number of persons confessing their faith in Christ than at any other time in his experience as a pastor.

The power was in the Living Lord, not in the sermon, or in the course of which that was the climax. Under God, the accessions to the church came because of personal work by officers and members of the home church. They rejoiced in the power of Christ to save because He is the Son of God. In all our evangelistic ministry the undergirding truth should be the Deity of Christ.

This kind of pulpit work also strengthens and heartens the man who believes in Christ. At a wedding rehearsal one of the ushers said to the visiting minister: "One night a few years ago you preached here about the Deity of Christ. I wish you to know that your message has helped me every day since. It is easier for a man to keep going straight when he is sure of Christ as the Son of God."

At times it is good to preach doctrine indirectly. In a series at night the pastor can deal with seven of the texts where our Lord uses the words "I am." To the original hearers, with their Old Testament background, the words would suggest Deity. In the Book of Exodus, as elsewhere, I AM is a title for the Eternal.[15] To us as Christians the seven passages indicate various

[14] John 20:31.
[15] Exod. 3:14; cf. John 8:58; Rev. 1:17c.

ways in which the Lord Christ does for us men what God alone can do. Who but He would dare to employ such figures about Himself?

The title of the series may be "The Sevenfold I Am," or else "Christianity is Christ." Such a sentence may appear at the top of the printed list, and at the beginning of every sermon. On the card as printed the texts below need not be given. But if they are, they should encourage the laymen to read the Fourth Gospel with the eyes of love, so as to see in chapter after chapter the face of the Redeemer.

The Food of the Hungry Soul ....John   6:35
The Secret of Christian Radiance.................John   8:12
The Doorway into the Abundant Life ....John   10:7
The Gentleness of Christ's Leadership............John   10:14
The Beginning of the Life Everlasting ....John   11:25
The Christ of Christian Experience ....John   14:6
The Secret of Abiding Fruitfulness ....John   15:1

In any such sermon the appeal should be largely to the imagination. What the parables are in the other Gospels, these allegories are in St. John. If the resulting messages are to be clear and strong, the man in the pulpit needs to interpret. He should translate each figure into fact, and then preach the fact in the light of the figure. Needless to say, that is difficult to do well. Everyone knows what the Lord Jesus means when He says that He is the Bread of God, but it is not easy to put the idea into words. However, if the sermons are well wrought, they will bring a blessing to every hearer.

On the Sunday following the series there may be a message about the Christ of the Cross. Through Him the power of God is ever at work in the hearts of sinful men. The text may be: "I, if I be lifted up from the earth, will draw all men unto me.

This he said, signifying what death he should die." [16]   The topic may be "The Magnetic Power of Christ."   The power that draws us men is in Him, not His Cross.   While that is a means of grace, the grace itself is in Christ.   With Him as subject the text begins, and with Him as object the holy words conclude. In the center is the Cross, as the magnet through which He draws us sinners to God.   Herein lies mystery:

> I know not how that Calvary's Cross
> A world from sin could free;
> I only know its matchless love
> Has brought God's love to me.[17]

All these messages about Christ should help to prepare the way for Easter with its Gospel of the Risen Lord.   That is a subject to which we shall return.   Meanwhile we should remember that around these two foci—the Cross and the Throne—the faith of the New Testament revolves, and so does apostolic preaching. Would that it were so everywhere today!

A sermon about Christ should be clear, kind, persuasive. Somewhere in the service, if not at the close of the sermon, there should be a clear, kind, winsome invitation for the unsaved hearer to accept Him as Saviour and Lord.   The appeal may be direct or indirect, and it may come in various ways.   Sometime during the sixty or seventy-five minutes that the laymen spends in the sanctuary he should come face to face with the Redeemer, and then hear Him say: "Behold, I stand at the door, and knock: if any man hear my voice, and open the door, I will come in to him, and will sup with him, and he with me." [18]

[16] John 12:32-33.

[17] Harry Webb Farrington; Harvard Prize Hymn, used by permission of the Hymn Society, New York, and Mrs. H. W. Farrington.

[18] Rev. 3:20.

THE APOSTLES' CREED

In many a church a series of popular sermons about the Apostles' Creed might help to solve the "problem of the evening service." The hour affords an opportunity to teach the basic facts of the Christian religion. In the Second Presbyterian Church of Louisville, at a time when the services at night were apparently a failure, a series on the Creed attracted a throng of eager listeners. Those messages have since appeared in print.[19]

The Apostles' Creed includes more than twenty affirmations of Christian belief. Hence it may be difficult to keep the series within bounds. One way to do so is to pass by certain clauses, for among the score of affirmations not all are of equal weight. Another plan is to prepare two separate series. That is probably the better way. Even so, there should be omissions.

The Creed naturally falls into the two main sections. In the first part the affirmations are objective; they have to do with God, not man. In the latter part the statements are more subjective; they concern man as well as God. In the first part the stress is on the Father and the Son; in the second the emphasis is on the Holy Spirit, and on man's experience of redeeming grace. The first part lends itself admirably to an evening series during the autumn; the second part, during the winter.

Whether there are two series, or only one, the opening sermon may be about "The Heart of the Apostles' Creed." It all clusters round the doctrine of the Trinity: "I believe in God, the Father .... and in Jesus Christ .... [and] in the Holy Ghost." Each of the other affirmations depends on the Fatherhood of God, the Lordship of Christ, and the Personality of the Holy Spirit. The fact of the Triune God undergirds all that we Christians believe.

In a message about the Trinity it is possible to secure clearness

---

[19] Teunis E. Gouwens, *Can We Repeat the Creed?* Abingdon-Cokesbury, 1938; cf. O. C. Quick, *Doctrines of the Creed,* Scribner, 1938.

and interest by calling attention to favorite hymns, such as "Holy, Holy, Holy" and "Come, Thou Almighty King." In the latter song the first stanza is about the Father; the second, the Son; the third, the Spirit; the fourth, the "Great One in Three." Such hymns do not prove the doctrine of the Trinity, or dissolve the veil of mystery, but they show that the truth is dear to the heart of the Christian Church.

For popular sermons about the Trinity, turn to the writings of Phillips Brooks. In a day when the doctrine was not highly esteemed in Boston and at Harvard, he did all in his power to uphold it. Partly because he boldly proclaimed the truth of the Triune God, the rector of Trinity Church became the most beloved clergyman of his day, and the most popular preacher at Harvard. Here is the basic philosophy of his pulpit work:

We are preaching the Trinity always. I should count any Sunday's work unfitly done in which the Trinity was not the burden of our preaching. . . . . The doctrine of the Trinity is the description of what we know about God. . . . . The truth is given to us, not to be lectured on but to be lived by. . . . . How fully are you living? Not how many doctrines do you hold, but how much of the life of God have you taken into your life? [20]

After the sermon about the Trinity there may be others on the Fatherhood of God, the Lordship of Jesus, the saving power of the Cross, the glory of Christ's Resurrection, the promise of the Second Coming, and the certainty of the Judgment. Surely this is enough for a popular series.

There may also be a message about the Virgin Birth.[21] In-

---

[20] *The Purpose and Use of Comfort,* Dutton, 1910, p. 228; cf. *Sermons for . . . . the Church Year,* Dutton, 1910; pp. 318-35; J. S. Stewart, *The Strong Name,* Scribner, 1941, pp. 251-60.

[21] Matt. 1:18, or Luke 1:35.

stead of using the truth as an ecclesiastical football, the pastor should avoid controversy. He can show that in the earthly life of our Lord everything else was unique, and that what two of the Gospels tell about His birth is in keeping with everything else that we know about Christ Jesus in the days of His flesh. Unfortunately, however, it would be easier to throw mud and stones at those who reject the teaching than to show what the Church believes, and why. Although the sermon is not easy to prepare, it will do good. Many a layman will be glad to learn what the New Testament teaches on the subject. He wishes to feel sure that it is still intellectually respectable to believe in our Saviour as born of the Virgin Mary.

Such preaching comes most fitly on Sunday evening. One reason is that the little boys and girls are at home in bed. Even so, the discussion should be relatively simple, as well as interesting. Many adults, who may be as good as gold, are not much given to logic. Others may not as yet be familiar with theological lore. In popular preaching, therefore, it is a safe rule to omit whatever one cannot illuminate. For instance, it would be out of the question for many a clergyman to prepare an edifying discourse on the clause, "He descended into hell," or "hades." Of course one might accept the simplest rendering, "He descended into the grave," but that is not what the Creed affirms. While the clause may have seemed clear enough to the holy fathers who drafted this form of sound words, the saying is obscure to many of us who now lead the saints in reciting the Apostles' Creed. According to a wise old saw, "When you cannot lift a stone, leave it alone." In the first part of the Creed there are more than enough clear, vital truths to keep a man busy during most of the Sunday evenings in the fall. Why then devote a sermon to what is neither clear nor vital? Keep on the main highway to the City of God!

The latter part of the Creed is short and compact. It may lead to a popular series, "The Meaning of Christian Experience." Since these messages are to come after New Year's, during the harvest season of the Christian Church, the emphasis may be somewhat evangelistic. Still there should be a good deal of popular teaching, for the best soul-winning sermons are indirectly doctrinal.

> How firm a foundation, ye saints of the Lord,
> Is laid for your faith in His excellent Word!

In the latter portion of the Creed every clause suggests a moving sermon. There should be messages about the Holy Spirit, as the power of God in the lives of men; the Holy Catholic Church, as the body of which Christ is the Head; the communion of saints, both on earth and in heaven; the forgiveness of sins, as the heart of religion on the human side; the resurrection of the body, as the truth shines out from the fifteenth chapter of First Corinthians; and the life everlasting, as it appears in the fifth chapter of Second Corinthians.

In such preaching the topics should be clear, not camouflaged. For instance, why conceal the fact that the sermon next Sunday evening is to be about the life everlasting? The text may be striking: "If this earthly tent of mine is taken down, I get a home from God, made by no human hands, eternal in the heavens." [22] In a day when the world has been at war, think of a soldier out on the field who hears the call to fold up his tent and start towards home. That is how the child of God should look upon death. It is the supreme adventure.

Nowhere is the Creed more Christian than in the climactic stress on the life everlasting. In a volume of noteworthy sermons

[22] II Cor. 5:1 (Moffatt).

James S. Stewart of Edinburgh makes this eternal truth seem vital. He says that in London during the first World War a regiment of soldiers was being entertained by a group of musicians. At the close of the evening hour the colonel requested one of the junior officers to express the gratitude of the troops. After he had spoken briefly, with grace and charm, as well as humor, he paused, and then said, in a quieter tone: "We are crossing to France and to the trenches, and very possibly, to death. Will any of our friends here tell us how to die?" [23] The silence was intense, for no one knew what to say or do. At length one of the musicians came forward and commenced to sing from Mendelssohn's *Elijah* the aria "O rest in the Lord." When the song had ceased, many eyes were filled with tears. More than one man had learned where to look for light on the last great mystery.

The simplicity of Stewart's preaching, here and elsewhere, reminds us that it is possible to be unduly ambitious. The temptation is doubly strong when one is dealing with a difficult doctrine. Instead of trying to compress into a single discourse all that the Bible tells about the resurrection of the body, or the life everlasting, the wise minister preaches about one aspect of the truth revealed in a shining text. When the subject is "Heaven as Home," [24] the appeal may be more to the heart than to the head. If so, the man in the pew will feel that God is near, and that He is good.

In a doctrinal sermon the call is for a popular interpretation of a high Christian truth, in order to answer the unspoken question of the hearer. The difficulty is that the man in the pulpit must know the heart hunger of his people. He must be able to understand what some part of the Bible teaches with reference to such

[23] *The Gates of New Life,* Scribner, 1941, p. 219.
[24] John 14:2.

a human need. Then he must be able to let the revealed truth shine out through his sermon so as to meet the human need. Is it any wonder that doctrinal preaching is difficult? Nevertheless, this is the need of the hour.

Listen again to Phillips Brooks, who is speaking to divinity students at Yale:

> The preachers that have moved and held men have always preached doctrine. No exhortation to a good life that does not put behind it a truth as deep as eternity can seize and hold the conscience. Preach doctrine, preach all the doctrine you know, and learn forever more and more; but preach it always, not that men may believe it, but that they may be saved by believing it.[25]

Such pulpit work ought to be in the best thought-forms of our day. The trend at present is toward "significant simplicity." Listen to Leslie D. Weatherhead, of the City Temple in London:

> In future, our preaching will have to be much more simple. So often ministers preach as though every member of the congregation had had a theological training. . . . . The greatest need in our preaching is to come down to brass tacks and show that Christ's message is life and power, beauty and harmony for daily living in the modern world.[26]

[25] *Lectures on Preaching,* Dutton, 1877, p. 189.

[26] *The Christian Century,* April 8, 1942, p. 453; see also H. H. Farmer, *The Servant of the Word,* Warrack Lectures, Scribner, 1942; Otto A. Piper, "Doctrine and Preaching," in *Reality in Preaching,* a symposium, Muhlenberg Press, 1942.

RECRUITING

From Christmas to Easter

Chapter V

PROCLAIMING THE GOSPEL

THE PLAN HERE IS TO PREACH FROM ST. LUKE ON SUNDAY MORN-
ings between the middle of December and the coming of Easter.
The idea is to announce each sermon separately, and not as part
of a series. The purpose each time is to bring the hearer face to
face with the Lord Jesus as He makes Himself known in this
beautiful book. If the man in the pew is not yet a Christian,
some one of these messages should lead him to accept the Saviour
and confess Him before men. If the hearer is already a believer
and a member of the home church, these sermons ought to increase his love for Christ and his zeal for the Kingdom. The
pastor's slogan for the period may be "Recruiting for Christ."

If all this is to follow, there needs to be careful preparation in
advance. Day by day throughout the autumn there should be
spade work in St. Luke, preferably starting with the Greek. The
unit of study ordinarily is the paragraph, as it appears in the
American Revised Version, or else Moffatt's *New Translation*.
There ought to be frequent reference to an exegetical commentary
or two, such as Plummer and Godet, or Easton and Manson.
All these studies should be practically completed before one begins
to use any part of the book in the pulpit.

In St. Luke, as in each of the other Gospels, each paragraph
has a message of its own. Almost without exception the central
teaching is about the Lord Jesus. In approaching any paragraph,
after one has learned exactly what it means, one should inquire,
"What do these words tell about Christ?" Then one ought to
ask, "What difference should this truth about Him make in the

heart and life of a typical layman in this parish?" After a few months of such fascinating study the minister should have in his files the preaching message of almost every paragraph in St. Luke. Then he can select for each Lord's Day a theme that will prove interesting and helpful to the persons whom the sermon ought to reach and move.

THE BEAUTY OF THE GOSPEL

The introductory message may be on the second Sunday before Christmas. Since everyone is likely to be thinking about "Fairest Lord Jesus," the topic may be "The Beauty of the Gospel." According to Rénan, the brilliant French skeptic and critic of literature, the Gospel of Luke is the most beautiful book ever written.[1] In this opening message one aim is to present the book so attractively that many a hearer will determine at once to make it his personal friend. Better still, the minister desires to present the Lord Jesus as He shines forth from these pages. The headings of the sermon may be somewhat as follows:

> The Beauty of the Saviour's Birth
> The Beauty of His Daily Life
> The Beauty of His Parables
> The Beauty of His Last Days on Earth

In preparing and in delivering such a sermon one needs to remember the maxim of F. W. Robertson, "Truth should be taught suggestively, not exhaustively." [2] Otherwise both preacher and hearer are likely to get lost in the woods. For example, in referring to the beauty of our Saviour's birth one need merely ask the friend in the pew to watch for the beauty in the opening chapters of St. Luke, especially in the parts that give the songs.

[1] See D. A. Hayes, *The Most Beautiful Book Ever Written*, Abingdon, 1923.
[2] S. A. Brooke, *Life and Letters of Fred. W. Robertson*, London, 1873, I, 153.

This portion of the sermon, like each of the other sections, ought to be short and interesting, as well as full of quiet beauty.

In dealing with the earthly life of our Lord the idea is to show the beauty of His personality. In His daily contacts with all sorts of people He showed us once for all the meaning of God in a life on earth. Especially in His dealings with the widow and the child, the poor and the helpless, our Lord revealed His gentleness and His power. Somehow or other it should be possible to phrase most of these ideas in the present tense, for He is still most wonderfully kind and gracious to the weakest and worst of men.

As for the parables, it may be sufficient to suggest that the friend in the pew learn where in St. Luke he can find the tale of the loving father, the rich fool, or the good Samaritan. Is there any reason why the layman should not commit some of these golden words to memory, so as to guide his growing boy in learning the truth in terms of beauty? At family prayers, also, why should not the father lead the household in reciting one or another of the parables from St. Luke?

The most precious chapters in the Third Gospel tell about the beauty of our Saviour's last days on earth. That beauty, alas, is for the eye of the believer. In the trial and death of the Redeemer there is an attraction only as those tragic hours are transfigured by the Resurrection. The climactic part of the book, as well as the most precious, is the closing chapter, which begins by telling how the Death of Christ brought gloom like that of the grave, and how the Risen Lord transformed the spirit of the disciples, so that their hearts burned with joy and hope.

Thus far we have been thinking about a single sermon,[3] which is to sound the keynote of all the morning pulpit work until after Easter. For the Sunday before Christmas the message

[3] The text may be Luke 4:22.

should be much easier to prepare, since the motif calls for painting with a smaller brush. From the song of the angelic host [4] we learn that religion often begins with a call to worship God. That is how the believer ought to start every day, and especially as he draws nigh to Christmas. When a man's religion and life begin with the upward look and a burst of song, there is likely to be erelong a vision from the throne of God.

In our text the ideal is that of a world at peace. The closing refrain is about "good will toward men." In modern speech the saying is "peace among men in whom He is well pleased," but why should we translate mystic poetry into halting prose? The angels tell us to sing about God, the nations, and ourselves. If we Christians praise God, strive for peace on earth, and love our fellow men, we surely have something of the spirit that brought the Saviour to Bethlehem. The topic may be "The Christmas Call to Worship." Somewhere in the service invite the unsaved hearers to accept Christ as Saviour and King.

A week later the subject may be "The Meaning of a Boy's Religion." [5] For a growing lad, being a Christian means becoming like the Lord Jesus when He was the same size. He alone is the Ideal Boy; He is God's revelation of what every lad should strive to become. In any such sermon one must be careful to speak of the Boy Jesus as entirely human. How otherwise could He live the Perfect Example of what a growing boy should strive to become?

The text contains three truths, which may appear in the order of time. From the day of his birth a little baby should have a sound body; that is the basis of everything else. More important, he should soon begin to have a well-trained mind; that will enable him to be useful among men. Most vital of all, he should

[4] Luke 2:14.
[5] Luke 2:40; cf. 2:52.

grow up with a loving heart, at peace with God and men. This is partly the meaning of the words, "the grace of God was upon him." Much of the truth here no one can fathom. Hence the facts about the early days of our Lord on earth should fill our hearts with a sense of mystery and wonder:

> I know not how that Bethlehem's Babe
> Could in the Godhead be;
> I only know the manger Child
> Has brought God's life to me.[6]

THE REALITY OF A MAN'S RELIGION

The next sermon may be about "Victory over Temptation." [7] This is a subject on which the minister should preach again and again, each time from a new text and a different point of view. As a rule the pastor stresses the perils of the man who is young, but surely older folk too have their temptations. When our Lord thrice met the devil on the proving ground, He was thirty years of age. So was Joseph at the supreme crisis of his career, and Albert Schweitzer when he began directly to prepare for his life work.

From another viewpoint the topic might be "Temptation as Life's Proving Ground." Before the new model of an automobile goes on the market there must be a series of tests out on a field with all sorts of driving conditions at their worst. In like manner the Father God permits a man to be tempted, in order to prove the reality of his religion. Of course there is a difference, for in testing a car both the manufacturer and the driver hope that it will stand up triumphantly, whereas in tempting a soul the devil wishes to see it falter and fall.

The devil is no ass; he has brains beyond our ken. When he

[6] Harry Webb Farrington; Harvard Prize Hymn, used by permission of the Hymn Society, New York, and Mrs. H. W. Farrington.
[7] Luke 4:1-2a.

finds a man hiding behind some Maginot Line supposed to be impregnable, the enemy of souls makes his assault from the flank, or else at the rear. Especially in dealing with our Saviour, the devil moved in unexpected ways. The first evil suggestion was to use the gifts of God in the service of self; the second, to make a vulgar compromise with the world; the third, to indulge in a spectacular display, as though He were a religious demagogue or charlatan.

The main question is how to repel the assaults of the devil. Our Lord shows the way, for His appeal is to the Book. At three different stages, in reply to the tempter, He quotes Deuteronomy. That eloquent book shows how the Children of Israel repeatedly met temptation in the wilderness, and how again and again they succumbed, because they did not rely upon God. In each quotation the stress falls on the word God. In much the same manner, years before, Joseph found strength by appealing to the Most High: "How then can I do this great wickedness, and sin against God?" [8]

Another sermon may be about "The Meaning of a Man's Religion." [9] Instead of treating the subject abstractly, why not study a typical case? The one before us now is that of a businessman, or rather, a politician. The emphasis, however, is on the Speaker, not the one whom He addresses. When our Lord says: "Follow me," He is inviting a man to be with Him in spirit, to become like Him at heart, and to keep moving forward. From the very first hour of a man's introduction to the Lord Jesus, life should be an up-to-date edition of *Pilgrim's Progress*.

Being a Christian today is far from easy. Occasionally one can soar; often one is able to run; at times one must plod through

[8] Gen. 39:9*c*.
[9] Luke 5:27*b*.

mud and sand.[10]   As with a motor car, the test of a man's religion comes when he must shift into low gear.   When others are falling by the wayside, can he keep on following the Lord Jesus in the steep ascent to heaven?   Yes, if like the man in the Gospel story the disciple has faith.   That means to be conscious of Christ's presence, to enjoy His fellowship, and to live according to His will.   As for the inspiration, it comes chiefly through the Cross.

If all this sounds like a beautiful theory from long ago, listen to the testimony of Sir Wilfred Grenfell when fifty-four years of age:

Feeble and devious as my own footsteps have been since my decision to follow Jesus Christ, I believe more than ever that this is the only real adventure of life. No other step do I even compare with that one in permanent satisfaction. I regret that I did not take it sooner. I do not feel that it mattered much whether I chose medicine for an occupation, or law, or education, or commerce, to justify my existence by working for a living, as every honest man should do. But if there is any one thing about which I never have any question it is that the decision to follow the Christ does for a man what nothing else on earth can do. Without stultifying our desires, it develops all that makes a man Godlike.[11]

THE PRACTICAL WORKINGS OF FAITH

Everyone knows that religion calls for faith, but what does that mean?   In a sense it is the human side of religion; if grace is divine power for man's need, faith is human weakness laying hold on that power.   But why deal with the subject theoretically when we have before us a clear example of how faith works in the experience of a practical man? [12]   Elsewhere in the Bible we

[10] Isa. 40:31.

[11] *A Labrador Doctor* (Autobiography), Houghton Mifflin, 1919, p. 429.

[12] Luke 7:9; cf. H. E. Fosdick, *The Meaning of Faith,* Association Press, 1917.

run across this word faith in various connections, all of them religious; here the emphasis is practical, for faith simply means trusting God.

The subject of the sermon may be "The Man at Whom Jesus Marvels." Twice in the days of His flesh our Lord is said to have marveled: once at men's unbelief,[13] and again at a man's faith. The amazing fact just now is not that a strong man should believe but that his brand of faith should be rare. On the human level this Roman captain is a man of might. In contrast with those about him the centurion is a person with authority. Among his soldiers, as well as his servants, his word is law. But in Christ this leader of men beholds power in a realm where an officer in the Roman army is as helpless as a babe. This is why the centurion intercedes for the servant who is dear. Why should not the masterful man in the pew give himself now to this same Strong Son of God?

The following Sunday there may be a message about "The Way to Hear a Sermon."[14] The suggestion comes from the pastor of the First Christian Church at Johnson City, Tennessee, Joseph H. Dampier,[15] who in turn quotes from a message by George Whitefield, "Directions on How to Hear Sermons." The young brother suggests that Whitefield's power over his hearers may have been due in part to the fact that he told them how to listen to sermons:

1. I direct or intreat you to come to hear them, not out of curiosity, but from a sincere desire to know and do your duty. . . . .
2. A second direction I shall lay down for the same purpose, is, not only to prepare your hearts before you hear, but also to give diligent

[13] Mark 6:6a.
[14] Luke 8:18a.
[15] A unique series of articles in *The Christian Standard*, Cincinnati; see the issue for February 1, 1941.

heed to the things that are spoken whilst you are hearing the Word of God. . . . .

3. [I beseech you] not to entertain any the least prejudice against the minister. . . . .

4. As you ought not to be prejudiced against, so should you be careful not to depend too much upon a preacher, or think of him more highly than you ought to think. . . . .

5. Make a particular application of every thing that is delivered to your own hearts. . . . .

6. If you would receive a blessing from the Lord, when you hear His Word preached, pray to Him, both before, in, and after every sermon to endue your minister with power to speak, and to grant you a will and ability to put in practice what he shall shew forth from the Book of God to be your duty.[16]

The next subject may be "The Best Place to Work for Christ." [17] Here once again is a concrete case, which embodies an abiding principle. The man before us is a new convert who wishes to become a permanent follower of the Master. In modern terms, this may mean that the young man wishes to enter the theological seminary. At a time when zealous workers are striving to enlist the youth of the Church for leadership as ministers, it seems strange that our Lord does not accept such a volunteer. To him the Master says, in effect: "The best place for you to win recruits is back at home as a layman."

Ofttimes the hardest place to begin doing personal work for Christ is at home, among relatives and friends. It may be that they know too much about one's past. At any rate, when the Lord Jesus bids the man begin at his home, he publishes the news throughout the entire city. Meanwhile the preaching message is that every believer should strive to win for the Saviour

[16] *The Doctrines of the Gospel,* Eighteen Sermons, London, 1739, Sermon X. Such ideas would need to be adapted today.

[17] Luke 8:39; cf. Mark 5:18-20.

the persons whom he knows best and loves most. Would that each parish now had a band of such personal workers!

There is likewise need of a sermon about "Christ's Cure for the Inferiority Complex." [18] In the case before us there is a physical cause. The nature of the woman's malady, as well as the dwindling away of her money, seems to have made her as sensitive as a shrinking violet. But when by faith she touched the hem of Jesus' garment she felt within her body the influx of healing power. When He bade her step forth, she forgot about her former modesty and shame; from that time forward she must have been a new woman. In short, when a person finds in the Lord Jesus a new center of life, the old inferiority complex should give way before new peace and assurance.

Still more directly evangelistic is the subject "The Cost of Being a Christian." [19] Sometimes the easy way to handle a familiar text is to explain its meaning, part by part. This one suggests four lines of thought. First, a man's religion starts with an act of decision: "If any man will." In the Greek this word is strong; it means to set one's heart, to be determined. Hence it is the fitting response of the bride at the marriage altar: "I will." Again, being a Christian calls for a spirit of unselfishness. "To deny oneself" means to cease striving to have one's own way. While it may be necessary, it is never enough, to give up pennies and nickels, or shreds and patches of time. What the Lord Jesus wishes most of all is the giving up of self.

Still further, being a Christian leads to a spirit of sacrifice. To "take up his cross daily" is to do for Him on the human level something like what the Lord Christ did in God's name for us on Calvary. Last of all, at least in this text and sermon, being a Christian leads to a life of service. Here again is the

[18] Luke 8:48; cf. II Cor. 5:17.
[19] Luke 9:23; cf. Matt. 16:24.

Master insisting that to be a disciple means daily progress in the practical art of being helpful. Since in the days of His flesh He went about doing good, the man who follows Him now in faith needs to be an apostle of kindness.

In a printed message that is worth the cost of the entire book,[20] William M. Clow puts his chief stress on "taking up the cross." He says that we Christians often confuse three familiar words: "burden," "thorn," and "cross." According to the Bible a burden is "the inevitable care and strain of earthly life." A thorn refers to "the experience of a keener anguish," about which a person almost never speaks to others. Both "the burden and the thorn are universal, and they are inescapable," whereas "the cross is not universal, and it can be escaped." "Your cross is something that you can take up or you can refuse." To take up the cross daily and then to bear it gladly, not because one must but because one can, is "The Mark of the Disciple." This is the topic of Clow's discourse. Is it any wonder that some of us look up to him as the most helpful of twentieth century preachers?

But surely this kind of evangelism is strange, especially if it comes not long before Easter. How can one win recruits by stressing the cost and difficulty of being a Christian? The answer is that this was the way of the Lord Jesus. He never gained a single recruit by appealing to a man's weakness rather than his strength. Rather did He dissuade everyone who had not first stopped to reckon up the cost. If such a heroic method gained comparatively few recruits, those who rallied to His call were faithful unto death. Who follows in their train?

THE RESPONSE TO THE GOSPEL

Now we are coming into the mountain country of the Third Gospel. Here we find the Parables, which have to do chiefly with

[20] *The Cross in Christian Experience,* Doran, 1908, pp. 231-42.

the grace of God to the needy and helpless. As a rule, these tales stress the positive, but once in a while the lesson is by contrast, to heighten the effectiveness of the surrounding Gospel. In the parable before us now the chief character is a rich man,[21] who seems to have been "self-made," and to have fallen in love with his maker. He voices a practical philosophy that has become common in our land: to live for things, not God; for self, not others; for time, not eternity. At the end of the story, when he has to leave all the things for which he has labored, his soul is bankrupt. Let that be the subject, "The Bankruptcy of the Soul."

In the Gospel of St. Luke the best-known chapter is the fifteenth. Nowhere in the Bible is there a richer field for evangelistic preaching. For instance, the first two parables suggest a sermon about "The Joys of the Soul Winner."[22] In fact, the message of all three parables is the gladness of the one who finds lost treasure. Needless to say, the reference is to the soul that has lost the way to God. With such inspiration from the pulpit, Sunday after Sunday, more than one church officer or godly woman will resolve to become like the shepherd, or the housemother, whose joy spread throughout the whole community. Why should it not be so today in every parish church?

There is likewise need of a message about "The Forgiveness of Sins." [23] As the experience of the prodigal makes clear, sin is a man's way of putting himself out of right relations with God and everyone else, including himself. In our text, however, the emphasis is on the father, not the son, and on forgiveness, not sin. What, then, is forgiveness? It is the Father's way of bringing His erring child back into right relations with

[21] Luke 12:20. In the dictionary, study the roots of the word "bankrupt."
[22] Luke 15:7, 10.
[23] Luke 15:22-24.

the One whom the son ought to love most of all. If the sin starts with a man, the forgiveness starts with God.

Instead of stating these facts abstractly, however, the Lord Jesus presents them in the form of a word picture that appeals to the eye of the soul. What, then, does He mean by the kiss and the robe, the ring and the shoes, as well as the feast in the old farm home? All of these Oriental symbols mean that the father has forgiven and forgotten, that he proposes to treat the wanderer henceforth as an honored son and not as a servant. Even before the son has time to say that he is sorry for his sins, the father shows him and everyone else the meaning of forgiveness. In order to understand this truth, one needs to have the experience of being pardoned and cleansed at the foot of the Cross.

In a sense it is easier to prepare a sermon about one of the ten lepers. If so, the stress ought to be on the Lord's approval of the man who returned to give thanks; and the subject may be "The Christian Spirit of Gratitude." [24] This is what President C. F. Wishart of Wooster College, Ohio, would term "Being a Gentleman with God." [25] A gentleman trusts the one with whom he is dealing, is ready to receive a favor that he cannot repay, and is worthy of note for his expression of gratitude. Incidentally, this is a fairly accurate picture of the ideal pastor for today.

After a brief introduction, the sermon may bring out some of the Christian's reasons for gratitude to God. Any of us has reasons far more wondrous than those of the leper who went out of his way to give thanks. Him the Lord Jesus restored to health and a place of standing among his fellow men. To

[24] Luke 17:17.
[25] See *The Unwelcome Angel and Other Sermons*, Westminster Press, n.d., pp. 103-13.

each of us who believe in Christ, God has granted the pardon of sins deadlier by far than leprosy. He has even given us the right to become His heirs in the home on high. "Praise God from whom all blessings flow!"

Over against such a lofty ideal is the black fact of ingratitude. The prevalence of this evil once led Clarence E. Macartney, of Pittsburgh, to preach about ingratitude as "America's Favorite Sin." Since he employed the topic for an evening sermon, he kept his prospective hearer guessing. The text proved to be from the life of Joseph.[26] Such a negative approach, occasionally, tends to heighten the effect of the messages that come before and after, being laden with Good News about the love of God.

When we confess our sins, do we often include ingratitude? Or are we like the nine lepers who were too busy to come back and thank the Lord Jesus? Among so-called respectable folk one out of ten would be a high average of thanksgivers. The majority of us are as ungrateful to God as we are indifferent to men.

Even the minister is not immune. In a certain home year after year the spare room was ready to receive any Protestant clergyman, regardless of denomination. As an honored guest he was free to tarry for days or weeks, with no thought of payment for lodging and meals. Sometimes a complete stranger would bring his wife, and one brother also had his canary bird in its cage. Among those who came and went, not one in a score ever wrote a letter or note of thanks, and not a single one sent the hostess a book or other token of remembrance.

As a rule, the cause was sheer thoughtlessness, if not ill breeding. With few exceptions those men were devout, and at heart they were kind. In later years when the housemother had no guest chamber, no hired servants, and no money to purchase

[26] Gen. 40:23.

extra food for entertaining angels unawares, she would often look back on those passing friends and offer a prayer of thanksgiving for the blessings they had brought her and the children. Even so, each of those ministers should have pondered the lines of Wordsworth about

> . . . . That best portion of a good man's life,
> His little, nameless, unremembered acts
> Of kindness and of love.[27]

As a rule, the man in the pulpit will accomplish more if he stresses the positive note of thanksgiving. The person who lives in the spirit of the fourth chapter of Philippians will not be lacking in gratitude to God or men. It may be no accident that our English word "thank" comes from a root meaning to think. The thoughtful man is thankful, and vice versa. Perhaps one reason why there is a world of gratitude among many who are poor is that they have abundance of time to think. As the lily grows out of muck in the swamp, so does the rarest grace often flourish where we least expect. Is it not the privilege of the Christian pastor to foster the growth of such lilies?

More directly evangelistic is the message about "The Meaning of Conversion." [28] Here the minister can stress the need today of adult evangelism. The man in Jericho must have been of middle age; perhaps he was older. He was the head of a household and well established in business. Notwithstanding all that certain phychologists say about the binding force of habit, this mature man became a Christian. He accepted Christ as his Saviour and started doing the will of God in business. Hence another topic might be "The Conversion of a Businessman," though really he was a politician.

---

[27] "Tintern Abbey."

[28] Luke 19:9*a*, or 19:10; see James Reid, *The Victory of God*, Hodder & Stoughton, London, 1933, pp. 76-86.

The use of money affords an acid test of a man's religion. In the case before us three facts witness to the reality of the transformation: he now thinks in terms of Christ, expresses his loyalty by the use of money, and thus becomes a different sort of human being. Hitherto he has been a social liability; henceforth he will be a community asset. Who but Jesus Christ can bring about such a change in the heart and life of one who is no longer young? "How can a man be born when he is old?" The answer is, through Christ.

In the Gospel of Luke there are countless other opportunities for sermons that win souls. But we have already looked at more than enough passages to keep a man busy on Sunday mornings until the beginning of Holy Week, a period that we shall consider separately. Meanwhile, if we glance back we shall see that by choosing a paragraph here and another one there it is easy to journey through a single Gospel and secure variety of materials, as well as abundance of spiritual food.

In such a course of sermons the emphasis ought to be more and more evangelistic. Fortunately, there are many interesting approaches to the City of Mansoul. First at one gate and then at another, sooner or later the man who perseveres with preaching the Gospel should gain admittance to introduce Christ as Saviour, and then make clear what steps are needful in order to unite with the church.

Strange as it may seem, soul-winning sermons of the right sort are meat and drink to the noblest saints in the congregation. Never do their hearts burn within them quite so much as when they hear the old, old story told in a form that seems new and strange. If any pastor, therefore, is wondering how he can strengthen and deepen the spiritual life of God's people, and at the same time add to the number of those who are being saved, let him seriously consider preaching his way here and there through the Gospel of St. Luke, or else St. John. Then both the veteran believers and the newer converts will be ready to welcome the approaching sermons about the Death and the Resurrection of Christ as Redeemer and King.

In the average congregation at present the best time for preaching to the unsaved and the unchurched is at the regular Sunday morning service. By actual count there are in attendance more persons not yet in vital touch with the Saviour and His Church than at any other hour of worship. Ordinarily there is no reason why the approach to these friends may not be somewhat indirect. Instead of announcing that there will be a series of revival sermons, why not simply make it clear that between Christmas and Easter all the messages on Sunday morning will be from the most beautiful book ever written? The spirit throughout should be that of the Crusader's Hymn, "Fairest Lord Jesus."

Week after week, as Christ makes Himself known through the sermon, each time in a different fashion, the friend in the pew should come face to face with the only One who can bring him pardon, cleansing, and peace. It still pleases God to save us mortals through "the foolishness of preaching." [29] As for the power that causes the transformation within the soul of a man, the source is in the Saviour and His Cross: "If any man be in Christ, he is a new creature: old things are passed away; behold, all things are become new." [30]

[29] I Cor. 1:21.

[30] II Cor. 5:17; this is the classic New Testament chapter about the Death of Christ.

Chapter VI

STRESSING THE CROSS

DURING HOLY WEEK THE SERMONS MAY BE FROM THE CLOSING chapters of St. Luke. The title of the series may be "The Drama of the Cross," with the first act on Palm Sunday and the last on Easter. At Oberammergau the entire drama falls within these two limits. In the local church, also, year after year, there can be a sort of Passion Play. The various messages ought to bring out the meaning of those final acts in the drama of redemption.

Another name for the series might be "The Journey to the Cross." [1] At present we are to think about still a third heading, "Conscience at the Cross." Before we turn directly to the series, however, we should consider what to do on Palm Sunday.

THE MESSAGE OF PALM SUNDAY

The day that marks the beginning of Holy Week may call for a message about Christ as King. In a city pulpit the subject may be, "When Christ Comes to Middletown." [2] As on the first Palm Sunday, He longs to rule over every city that He died to redeem. In our own city on the first day of the week He is present at the church; within the sanctuary, if nowhere else, He ought to have His way. Most of all is He anxious to reign in the heart that is open to receive Him as Lord. In a village or rural church the same principles would apply, but

---

[1] See James Stalker, *The Trial and Death of Jesus Christ,* Doran, 1894; G. Ray Jordan, *Why the Cross?* Abingdon-Cokesbury, 1941; F. K. Stamm, *In the Shadow of the Cross,* Macmillan, 1941.

[2] Luke 19:38.

there the topic might be "The Lord in Our Village," or "Christ in Our Community Today."

Another plan, still more worthy, is to set apart the morning of Palm Sunday for a sermon about the Cross. If the minister is in charge of a circuit, or of any congregation with preaching only on Sunday mornings, there should be prior to Easter a sermon about the Death of Christ. Otherwise God's people might attempt to celebrate the Resurrection without having thought much about Calvary. In the pulpit, as in life, how could there be an Easter without a Cross?

In the Third Gospel, as in each of the others, the climactic events are the Death and the Resurrection of Christ. The two are as inseparable as night and day, or death and life. When we put Calvary and Easter together, and look upon them in the light of our Lord's Deity, we behold the mystery of redemption. In the pulpit many of the fathers stressed the Cross rather than the Resurrection. Now certain of the sons are proclaiming the Living Christ, with comparatively little about the Dying Saviour. Why should not every Christian minister preach the Gospel as it stands?

Whatever the theme of the sermon, Palm Sunday is the beginning of Holy Week. In this connection it is good to remember that the deadliest of our American wars came to its end on a Palm Sunday. In *Abraham Lincoln: The War Years,*[3] by Carl Sandburg, one of the ablest chapters bears the heading, "Palm Sunday of '65." On April 9, the commanders of two opposing armies in Virginia signed terms of peace. Never have the conditions of an armistice been more magnanimous, and never has the spirit of the vanquished leader been more Christlike.

[3] Four vols., Harcourt, Brace, 1939; cf. Douglas S. Freeman, *Rober E. Lee,* four vols., Scribner, 1934.

Another chapter by Sandburg is still more poignant, for the title is "The Calendar Says Good Friday." On April 14, 1865, Lincoln was shot, after he had spent his last days in efforts to avert further bloodshed. He had also been striving to formulate honorable terms of peace: in the flag of the Union he longed to see every star that stood for a state in the South. At heart he was a lover of peace, not war.

After his death, the body was taken to Springfield, Illinois, for burial. There is a tradition that while the funeral cortege was passing through the main street a colored woman held aloft her little son and whispered: "Take a long look, my boy; he died for you."

A more recent illustration has to do with life, not death. Late in 1917 the British troops wrested the Holy Land from the Turks, and on December 11 the commanding officer, Field Marshal Viscount Allenby, entered the Holy City on foot.[4] He did not wish to pose as a conquering hero, for he was a friend of the liberated people. In much the same spirit during the next few years the British authorities practically transformed the "Holy City." As long as they were in control, it was almost a model of order and sanitation. Would that it had been so in the South during our own years of so-called Reconstruction.

The reference to these facts in modern history raises an important question. Is it wise for the minister, whether North or South, to employ in the pulpit materials taken from the War of 1861-65, and conflicts more recent? Is it not wiser to draw facts from sources less likely to arouse dissent? Why start cross-currents of thought and feeling? Why draw attention away from the Lord Jesus as Saviour and King?

The answer is that much depends on the local background.

---

[4] See Sir Archibald Wavell, *Allenby, A Study in Greatness,* Oxford Press, 1941, p. 230.

Without being cowardly and insincere the minister can be kind and tactful. In South Carolina a passing allusion to Robert E. Lee or Stonewall Jackson would cause no hearer to cease thinking about Christ. In Ohio a reference to Lincoln or Lee would cause no elderly man to frown or shake his head. But when it comes to speaking about General William T. Sherman in South Carolina, or General John H. Morgan in Southern Ohio, it is wise to let the dead past bury its dead.

Any such illustration may foment sectional bitterness. Even if there are no hard feelings, the facts may call attention away from the Cross. For instance, while reading the last few paragraphs, who has kept his mind fixed on the Redeemer? In all our preaching, including the illustrations, especially in Holy Week, the Lord Jesus should be at the center, and every eye should be fixed upon Him.

War at times may be a tragic necessity. Nevertheless, Christ is the Prince of Peace. That is the Christian ideal, and never does the truth shine out more clearly than in the Cross and the Resurrection. The practical conclusion is obvious: in the pulpit the minister should employ historical materials that will throw light on the meaning of the Christian religion, but he should not introduce anything that will call attention away from Christ. When in doubt, don't!

On the evening of Palm Sunday the message may be about "The Religion of the Upper Room." [5] The architecture of the home church may suggest something of the sort. If so, the minister and the people alike should look on the place of worship much as Peter and John regarded the Upper Room. For Christians today, as for the disciples of old, the meetinghouse is a symbol of public worship, which comes to its height in the Lord's Supper. The Upper Room is the place where the Holy

[5] Luke 22:12; cf. Acts 2:1ff.

Spirit bestows His power. At the sanctuary, in response to united prayer, He is waiting to equip believers with power for evangelism at home and missions abroad. In both realms of Christian service the dynamic comes from Christ. On the evening of Palm Sunday, therefore, strike the note that is to sound forth in every sermon until Easter morn: "The Son of God died for us men and for our salvation."

THE SERIES ABOUT THE CROSS

In the series during the week there may be five sermons about "Conscience at the Cross." The plan in view calls for five case studies, each of which has to do with a man's conscience in the presence of the Dying Redeemer. Conscience is the God-given power that shows a man what is right and what is wrong, impels him to do the right and not the wrong, approves him when he has done the right, and rebukes him when he has done the wrong.

Such is the ideal, but it takes no account of sin. What water does to the works of a watch, sin does to the conscience of a man. Under a different figure, it is seared, or branded, as with a hot iron.[8] Never do the weird workings of conscience appear so awful as in the presence of the Cross, where we behold the contrast between the purity of the Redeemer and the sins of other men, one by one.

Under the shadow of Calvary, as everywhere else in life, conscience is personal. Instead of dealing with it abstractly, or en masse, the man in the pulpit should look upon it much as the physician observes a patient's heart through the fluoroscope. In the sermon, as in the Gospel records, the secrets of the human heart should be revealed. It was so in 1930 and in 1934 at the Passion Play. When "Peter" was denying his Lord, or when

[8] I Tim. 4:2b.

"Judas" was selling Him to death, each of us who beheld the action felt prompted to exclaim: "Lord, is it I? Is that my sin?"

Such preaching searches the heart. According to a shrewd old Scotsman, the way to do that is simple: "Remember your own sins and charge them on the congregation; you will hit every man in the house." But be careful not to hurl a boomerang. First be sure that your own sins have been forgiven. Who wishes to hear exhortations from a present-day Judas, still burdened with the weight of his guilt?

The Monday evening sermon about Judas in the presence of Christ [7] should be dramatic, for the facts are so. The essence of many a serious drama is a struggle in the soul. At the Metropolitan Museum of Art in New York City there is a statue by George G. Barnard, "The Struggle of the Two Natures of Man." The same motif dominates the story *Dr. Jeckyll and Mr. Hyde* by Robert Louis Stevenson, and still more moving is the struggle in the soul of Shakespeare's *Macbeth*.

The modern name for such a state of mind is the "divided self." While the phrase is of recent vintage, the fact is as ancient as Adam and Eve. For a discussion of the "split personality" turn to *The Varieties of Religious Experience* by William James.[8] But in the sermon keep psychology out of sight and focus the hearer's attention on Judas as he stands over against the Saviour.

The topic may be "The Conscience of Judas." The introduction may show how the Lord Jesus appeals to the heart of a man who is young. When Judas became a disciple, he seems to have been on the threshold of young manhood. As long as the cause of Christ met with success and acclaim, he appears to have been loyal. Thus the early experiences of Judas with our Lord bring to

[7] Luke 22:5.
[8] Longmans, Green, 1902, chap. VIII.

view the sunlit hemisphere of his divided self, for what goes on beneath the shadows is largely in the realm of the subconscious.

The first main part of the sermon may have to do with our Lord's concern for a young man of promise. Usually we think of Judas as a monster of iniquity, a fiend incarnate, but to his comrades in the school of Christ that young man seemed to possess both ability and charm. He was one of the leaders in the band whom the Lord Jesus chose as future apostles. Among the twelve Judas was the treasurer. Near the Cross, when they learned that one of their number was a traitor, no one of them suspected Judas.

By way of contrast, the central part of the sermon may show how the lure of money leads a man to betray the Son of God. In the heart of Judas other motives doubtless combined with greed; a man's reasons for doing wrong are seldom so simple as our sermons make them seem. Still it is wise to fix the hearer's gaze on the sin that has to do with money.

As an example, take the record about the sons of Jacob,[9] who for twenty pieces of silver sold their younger brother into slavery. The wrongs those men perpetrated against Joseph were like "The Sins that Crucified Christ": envy, lying, greed, politics, murder. In the Old Testament account note the part of Judah, who suggested the sale of his young brother. The word Judah in Hebrew is the same as Judas in Greek. The difference between the two men was that Judah repented, whereas Judas committed suicide.

The latter part of the message ought to be climactic, for it has to do with the closing hours in the earthly life of Judas. In the struggle between God and mammon, the decision was against the Most High, and Judas sold his Saviour. Then there swept over the soul of the traitor a flood of remorse, and he attempted

[9] Gen. 37:28; cf. 44:18-34.

to give the blood money back to those who had bought his soul. When they refused to touch the polluted silver, the man who had chosen it rather than Christ went out and hanged himself.

The drama of the Cross may lead the minister to speak for a few minutes about suicide, which is the antithesis of Calvary. Think of Christ nailed to the Cross by sinners whom He is dying to redeem, and of Judas suspended from a tree because of his share in causing the Son of God to die. Think also of the loved ones back at the home of the disciple, who have been tempted to boast about their boy, because he has gone into the ministry of the Gospel. How can they ever recover from their shame when they learn that he has betrayed the Lord Jesus and then committed self-murder?

If the Cross is the supreme symbol of courage and sacrifice, the suicide of a man in his senses is the extreme example of cowardice and selfishness. These are among the blackest sins of which Judas was guilty. Without bitterness the Apostle Peter later speaks of his dead classmate as having reserved for himself a place in hell.[10] These facts in the Bible stand as a silent warning, a danger signal whenever a follower of Christ is tempted to be untrue.

The sermon about "The Conscience of Peter"[11] should be still more effective. Almost every man who knows the facts is full of sympathy for Peter. Like Judas, he was something of a divided self. The better part of him was loyal to Christ, and the real man in young Simon enabled him to become the leader of the apostolic band. But the baser part of Peter's personality caused him to shrink from the sneers of strangers, and even to deny his Lord. Then the rash young fellow tried to buttress up his lies with curses.

---

[10] Acts 1:25*b*. On suicide read Bunyan, *Pilgrim's Progress*, I, chap. 15.
[11] Luke 22:62.

If the treachery of Judas makes a man shudder, the sin of Peter should strike terror to the heart. For every one of us who follows in the footsteps of Judas, there may be a hundred who are like Peter. Except for the grace of God, any one of us might deny the Lord Jesus. But still there is hope for the weakest of us men who trust in Christ.

The difference between Peter and Judas is like that between mercy and doom. With the one man the grace of God won the victory and brought him life abundant, both on earth and in heaven. With the other the wiles of the devil prevailed and led to his death, without God and without hope in the world.

The sermon about Peter should make clear the meaning of Christian repentance, which leads to life, both here and hereafter. The New Testament employs two terms for repentance. The word that applies to Peter means "a change of mind," an "about-face." Christian repentance results in a personal transformation, for the sinner resolves that by God's grace he will henceforth live for God, not self.

The other term for repentance applies to Judas. It means to be sorry without turning to God. In other words, there must be more than mere feeling; the proof of a man's penitence should be practical. He must loathe his sin so much that he will turn away from it forever. Humbly should he do whatever he can to right the wrongs that he has committed, for true sorrow of soul issues in a life of service. Beginning with Pentecost the Apostle Peter brought forth fruits worthy of repentance.

When at last he died on a Roman cross, Peter asked that he be placed head downward, because he felt unworthy to die as his Lord had done. By faith he had long since reserved for himself a place in heaven. With him today in the Father's House is a host of sinful mortals whom he brought home to God by preaching the Cross.

The sermon about "The Conscience of Pilate" [12] has to do with a master politician. What he said about the Galilean was admirable: "I find no fault in this man." But what the Roman Governor did as judge was diabolical. If Pilate had felt that the charges against Jesus were valid, there might have been some excuse for having Him chastised. However mistakenly, a ruler of another type would have been consistent. But to be assured of Christ's innocence, to order that He be scourged, and then to decree that He be crucified—all of that was a travesty of justice.

Since the Victim was the Son of God, that scene was earth's darkest tragedy. But before we throw a stone at Pilate, let us ask if we too are not guilty of much the same sins. Whenever we are, says one of the most eloquent apostolic writers, we crucify to ourselves the Son of God afresh, and put Him to an open shame.[13]

With Pilate the controlling motive was fear. The vice of the politician is cowardice. What he says may be in line with the laws of God, but what he does belies his words. In such a case it is the deeds, not the words, that count for eternity. Even though the evildoer may have a "poker face," he cannot hide his feelings from God. Back of Pilate's deeds, causing his fear, was a black past. All the while he was standing face to face with the only One on earth who could have set him free from that past, and from all his guilty fears.

These facts are dramatic. At the Passion Play in 1930 and in 1934 the most moving scene was that in which our Saviour stood before the judgment seat of Pilate. On the stage eight hundred men and women, boys and girls, were hurling imprecations against the Prisoner who dared to style Himself the King of the

[12] Luke 23:4, 16.
[13] Heb. 6:6; cf. 10:29.

117

Jews. With diabolical vindictiveness the infuriated mob kept screaming: "Crucify Him! Crucify Him!"

In the face of those rioters, almost insane with fury, Pilate yielded. Reluctantly he consented to the death of the Nazarene. If the governor had delivered Him from the Cross, there might have been an uprising in Jerusalem, and then there would have been an inquiry at Rome. In such a crisis the politician looks out for himself. Before we find fault with Pilate, however, let each of us ask: "If I had stood in that judgment hall and had been forced to choose between the Man and the mob, would I have been true to my God or the victim of my fears?"

Such preaching ought to move the conscience: "'Tis man's perdition to be safe when for the truth he ought to die." While the man in the pulpit is speaking about the vacillation and the surrender of Pilate, the friend in the pew should be asking: "Lord, is it I? Is that my sin?" Today, as at Oberammergau, each of us should answer: "Yea, Lord, it is I."

At the Broadway Tabernacle in New York City, William M. Taylor once led every hearer to behold Christ before Pilate.[14] Erelong the searchlight from the pulpit fell upon the politician who was standing before the King of Kings. That is where every one of us will appear someday, to be judged according to the deeds done in the body. While it matters much what a man thinks of Christ, it also matters tremendously what Christ sees in a man. The Lord Jesus alone is able to read the heart. He only can "welcome, pardon, cleanse, relieve." The Christ of the Cross is able even to transform the soul of a coward and make him worthy to live forever with God.

Next we turn to Barabbas, who seems to have been a confirmed criminal. Through him we learn indirectly about "The Con-

---

[14] See *Contrary Winds*, Armstrong and Son, 1883, pp. 37-50.

science of Christ." [15] In the heart of our Saviour the Spirit of God led to the choice of the Cross. In place of Barabbas, who was unworthy to live, the Son of God was glad to die. By the mercy of God, that other man, who deserved to die, was free to live.

Here is "The Barabbas Theory of the Atonement." As in many another doctrine about God and men, this truth involves a paradox. In fact, Christianity as a whole is a series of apparent contradictions. Over against man's guilt is God's grace. While there is no proof that Barabbas accepted the Lord as Saviour, that is what he should have done. The truth of vital moment for every man today is that the Son of God was willing to die. Such a sermon should lead the friend in the pew to accept Him, here and now.

"Why Did Jesus Die?" When the writer was a young pastor in Pittsburgh, the church bulletin board once carried this topic. On her way to the parochial school a little girl stopped and spelled out the words. Then she exclaimed: "Those Protestants don't know why Jesus died!" Perhaps not, for who does? At any rate, on the next Lord's Day the people heard the old, old story. Sixty years previously, it had led Cecil Alexander to write the hymn "There is a green hill far away." Her aim was to guide little boys and girls in beholding the mystery and the wonder of the Cross:

> We may not know, we cannot tell,
>   What pains He had to bear;
> But we believe it was for us
>   He hung and suffered there.

The last of the five sermons may be the most appealing. The subject is "The Conscience of the Dying Thief." [16] The facts

[15] Luke 23:18.
[16] Luke 23:43.

119

afford materials for more than one message. Just now we are using them for a case study in adult conversion. The few words of our text come close to the heart of the Christian Evangel, for they show how the Christ of Calvary pardons the worst of sinful men. In the case before us there is no question about the enormity of the man's transgressions. Neither is there any opportunity for him to perform penance, or make restitution. All he can do is to throw himself on the mercy of the Dying Redeemer.

The thief was saved as he was dying. In modern terms, the clock was almost ready to strike twelve. In all the Bible there is only a single case of what we may call "death-bed repentance." There is one example, lest some sinful mortal should despair; only one, lest some wicked person should presume. It is possible for a man to be saved while he is gasping for the last breath, but that is not the normal way to get right with God.

In the sermon the emphasis is on adult conversion. In many a church it is possible for a man of middle age to attend divine services regularly for years without once hearing that there is hope for one who is no longer young. He may not have been guilty of insurrection and murder, but he should feel drawn towards the Saviour who pardoned the dying thief. In the sort of preaching that wins a man's allegiance, nothing is more moving than the kindness of the Cross.

The scene also sheds light on what lies beyond the grave: "Today shalt thou be with me in paradise." According to the Westminster Shorter Catechism, "The souls of believers are at their death made perfect in holiness, and do immediately pass into glory; and their bodies, being still united to Christ, do rest in their graves till the resurrection."

The statement is true, but the words of the text are more likely to move the heart. Where the Catechism speaks of "believers," collectively, the Lord Jesus has to do with the one dying sinner. That one, however, is typical of a host whom no man can number. The soul of the penitent thief was to go from earth to Paradise. That very hour he was to be with the Saviour in an abode of rest and beauty, and the same is true of everyone dying who trusts on the mercy of the Redeemer. Such facts once led Canon Liddon to deliver at St. Paul's in London a discourse that has become famous, "The First Five Minutes After Death." [17]

If we look back over the five sermons we shall note that each of them has to do with a man's response to Christ in the presence of the Cross. Especially towards the end of the series the emphasis ought to be on His power to change the climate within a man's soul. Through religion, says William James, the one who is "consciously wrong, inferior, unhappy" becomes consciously "right, superior, happy." The classic examples to whom the psychologist refers are Augustine, Bunyan, and Tolstoy.

The power to transform a sinner into a saint is in the Christ of the Cross. Why do Judas and Peter, Pilate and Barabbas, as well as the dying thief, appear in the Gospel records? Is it not because each of them came close to the Dying Redeemer? Whenever the heart of any such person responds aright, shifting sand becomes solid rock, a sinful mortal becomes an heir of heaven. But if conscience balks before the Christ of the Cross, there may be for the sinner naught save the fearful looking for of judgment. In every such sermon the vital question is, how does the hearer respond when his soul is exposed to the searchlight of the Cross?

THE GLORY OF EASTER

The sermons about "Conscience at the Cross" should prepare the way for Easter. Here we seem to be in a different world.

---

[17] *Forty-Two Sermons on Various Subjects*, London, 1886, No. 1,098.

Whereas the mood of the disciples at the Cross was one of gloom and despair, the spirit of those who believed in the Risen Lord was that of joy and hope. Hence the subject of the morning sermon may be "The Religion of Easter," [18] since the word Easter is only another name for Christianity. Of all the days in the year this one is most distinctly Christian. In fact, the spirit of Easter should carry over into every Lord's Day. According to the New Testament, the first day of every week celebrates the Resurrection of Christ.

The religion of Easter centers in a Person, not a place. Why, then, should believers in Christ quarrel about where He was buried and from whence He arose? Was it at Gordon's Calvary or the Church of the Holy Sepulcher? Perhaps it was neither, but whatever the place, it never was intended of God to be used as a shrine. The Gospel writers seldom concern themselves about any locality, for they fix our gaze upon the Living Christ. They exalt the Person who by His Death and Resurrection became the Redeemer of mankind. At heart the Creed of the Christian ought to be as simple as it is sublime. Christianity centers in the Living Christ.

The religion of Easter stresses life, not death. Why do more men come to church on this one morning than for any other two services in the Christian Year? Because, perhaps unconsciously, they yearn for light on what lies beyond these days of earth. Judging from their experiences in attending public worship at other times, they know that there is usually little or nothing about the life everlasting. But they feel that on this one morning only an artful dodger could fail to voice the Easter Hope.

Today there is special need of such Good News, for every

[18] Luke 24:5b-6a.

growing lad wonders how soon he will be called out to a training camp, and every mother is afraid her son will be slain on
some remote battlefield. Surely there is a need for sermons
about what lies beyond: "I believe in . . . . the forgiveness of
sins; the resurrection of the body; and the life everlasting."

The religion of Easter likewise calls for service, not enjoyment.
In the message of this glad day there are three imperative verbs.
The first is "Fear not"; "Trust God, see all nor be afraid." The
second is "Come"; the call is to worship the Living Christ. The
third is "Go"; spread the Good News; tell it to the man across
the street and the stranger beyond the sea. Worship and evangelism, adoration and missions, rejoicing in the sanctuary and
serving on the highway—all of these belong to the spirit of
Easter. Is it any wonder, therefore, that the harvest season of
the Christian Church comes to its height on this glad day?

At the evening service, or at vespers, the sermon may be on
"The Afterglow of Easter Day." [19] In view of world conditions
at present, there is a temptation to descant upon "The Lost
Radiance of the Christian Church." But the spirit of Easter is
positive rather than negative. The day calls for the Good News
of God, not the dark fears of man. The Gospel that dispels
doubt and fear comes from the Living Christ as He walks and
talks with the two disciples on the road to Emmaus. Above all
does He make Himself known in the breaking of bread.

As on the road to Emmaus, the Lord Jesus reveals Himself
today in the hour of worship. Whenever two or three are
gathered together—it may be two or three hundred, or else two
thousand—He is in their midst. Hence they should have burning hearts, as well as glowing faces. Especially should such be
the case at the Lord's Supper. Whenever the soul of the believer
is kindled at His altar, the life becomes luminous. The secret

[19] Luke 24:32.

of the Christian glow, therefore, is the indwelling presence of the Living Redeemer.

That experience on the road to Emmaus likewise shows how the Living Lord makes Himself known through the Bible. "Did not our heart burn within us, ... while he opened to us the scriptures?" The reading of the written Word is a vital part of public worship, as well as private devotions. Except when we celebrate the Sacrament, nothing else that we do in the sanctuary is more vital than the reading from God's Holy Book. In order to have a sunlit church, therefore, lead the laymen to use the Bible as the mirror in which they can behold the Living Christ. When they behold Him there, they should be transformed into His likeness.[20]

He makes Himself known, once again, in Christian service. Doing good is no substitute for public worship, but neither is public worship the equivalent of doing good. These two are as inseparable as the light and the heat of the sun. One reason for the spiritual glow among the early believers was that they began at once to share the Good News with others. If the two disciples had tarried in the village where they first beheld the glory of the Risen Lord, if they had tried to keep their discovery a secret, the light would have faded from their faces before the sun went down.

Joy unshared quickly wanes. Religion that does not shine soon ceases to be Christian. On the other hand, the more grace a man imparts the more he has to enjoy. When those two pilgrims hied forth to tell others about the Lord, their own hearts kept singing. From that day to this, wherever the Church has been worthy of note for evangelistic and missionary zeal, the members have had burning hearts and glowing lives. This truth

[20] II Cor. 3:18.

shines out from the books of E. Stanley Jones, notably *The Christ of the Indian Road.*[21]

Sometimes we Christians ask, "How can we 'maintain the spiritual glow'[22] that marked the Early Church? One answer is that we should begin preaching more about the Living Christ, and thus do away with our postmortem sermons. Too often have we spoken of Christ simply as One who lived far away and long ago. From James Denney, master theologian of yesterday in Scotland, we should have learned that "the Christian religion depends not on what Christ was, merely, but on what He is; not simply on what He did, but on what He does." Much the same note sounds forth today from Karl Barth: Christ is our Contemporary.

When we preach from the Gospels [says Denney], and see what Jesus was, and said, and did, and suffered, let us remember to make the application in the present tense. Never preach about the historical Christ; preach about the Living, Sovereign Christ. . . . . It is not because He lived, but because He lives, that we may have life also; it is not because the historical imagination is highly developed, so that we can make the evangelists' pages vivid, and be affected as by a fine scene in a drama—but because we confess with our mouth and believe in our heart that God raised Him from the dead—that we are saved. Faith always has its object here and now, and without faith there is no religion.[23]

This truth came to the present writer at the Church of the Holy Sepulcher in Jerusalem one morning before the sun had risen. Under the guidance of a friendly Dominican monk the Protes-

---

[21] Abingdon-Cokesbury, 1925.

[22] Rom. 12:11*b* (Moffatt).

[23] *Studies in Theology,* Hodder & Stoughton, London, 1895, p. 154—a strong book.

tant clergyman had gone into the chapel where the body of
Jesus is supposed to have lain between Calvary and Easter.
There on his knees, surrounded by strangers, and almost within
arm's length of the sacred slab that the others were adoring, he
was trying to worship God while a Roman priest was celebrating
the Mass. When at length he stumbled out into the open air,
he found himself murmuring: "The Living Christ was not there!
'They have taken away my Lord, and I know not where they
have laid Him!' " [24]

Just then the sunlight came streaming over the summit of
Mount Olivet, and the pilgrim exclaimed with joy: "My Lord
is here! He is Light, and Life, and Love! His mercy brightens
all the path in which we rove." This is why at the Sacrament
we gather round the Table to be with Him as our Divine
Host, and not round a tomb to remember Him as our Dead
Saviour. "I am he that liveth, and was dead; and, behold, I am
alive for evermore." [25]

> When morning gilds the skies,
> My heart awaking cries,
> May Jesus Christ be praised!

[24] John 20:13*b*.
[25] Rev. 1:18*a*.

INSTRUCTING

From Easter to Pentecost

Chapter VII

PRESENTING THE RISEN LORD

DURING THE SIX SUNDAYS AFTER EASTER THE MORNING SERMONS
may be about the post-Resurrection appearances of our Lord.[1]
If so, the stress should be on His interviews with the disciples.
Since the Biblical records are few, it may prove necessary to draw
from more than one Gospel. We have already looked at the
closing chapter of St. Luke. The last twelve verses in St. Mark
seem not to be genuine; they do not appear in the most ancient
Greek manuscripts. Hence we shall confine ourselves to the
closing sections of St. Matthew and St. John, as well as the
opening sections in the Book of Acts.

There need be no attempt to follow the order of events chrono-
logically. What concerns us now is the meaning and spiritual
value of each interview with the Risen Lord. During the forty
days prior to the Ascension, He held repeated conferences with
the disciples. Of course these human figures are interesting,
but we should fix our attention chiefly on the Living Christ.
Whenever He appears in the picture He ought to stand at the
center with the light of God shining full on that blessed Face.

THE MEANING OF THE NEW RELIGION

In a sense the Christian movement had a new birth at the
Resurrection. Like many another forward movement in the
Church that new beginning had to do with worship. Hence the
first morning sermon after Easter may be on "The Spirit of
Christian Worship." [2] Never on earth have the tides of devotion

[1] For a different trail at this season consult A. W. Blackwood, *Preaching from
the Bible*, Abingdon-Cokesbury, 1941, pp. 119-22.

[2] Matt. 28:16-17.

to the Lord Jesus risen higher than during the days following the Resurrection.[3] For the explanation of that power and joy we should look at the closing verses in St. Matthew. There we can see that Christian worship thrives in the atmosphere of evangelism and missions. These are two different aspects of Christian service: evangelism is Christian missions at home, whereas missions is Christian evangelism abroad. Each of them has much to do with worship.

The text shows the importance of the place where the brethren meet with the Living Lord. Theoretically we can worship God anywhere. Actually we can be in only one spot at a given time. For every person or group the ideal place of worship is where the Lord Jesus has appointed. Usually it is where we have met with Him before. The mountain in Galilee where He asked His disciples to assemble had doubtless been the scene of more than one ministerial "retreat," with the Lord as the Leader. In a day when such gatherings are common, our text would provide a starting point for the opening meditation.

Far more important than the place where we assemble is the Person whom we adore. "When they saw him, they worshipped him; but some doubted." They were all together in one place, but the only persons who received a blessing were those who could behold the Risen King. Today the purpose of our gathering together in the House of God is to be with the Living Christ, that we may confess our sins and voice our love for Him. In songs and prayers we acclaim Him as King; in the reading of the Scriptures and in the sermon He makes Himself known as our Saviour and Lord. Above all at the celebration of the Sacrament our worship should center in Christ as the Son of the Most High God.

[3] See Fr. Heiler, *The Spirit of Worship,* Hodder & Stoughton, London, 1928, p. 21.

The next sermon may be about "The Supreme Court in Religion."[4] In all matters relating to belief and conduct, who has the right to speak the last word? To the majority of us Protestants the Holy Scriptures are the final court of appeal, "the only infallible rule of faith and practice." The Roman Catholics and others insist that "the Holy Church throughout all the world" is superior even to the written Word of God. The Friends, or Quakers, and other mystical saints of God prefer to follow their loftiest feelings, especially in the way of "the inner light." The Unitarians and kindred groups insist that the reason of man ought to be paramount.

In a vital sense each answer above is correct in what it affirms. The reason and the feelings, the Church and the Bible, are channels that God uses in making known His holy will. But even at best these are only means of grace; the grace itself is in Jesus Christ. Chiefly through the Scriptures, but likewise in those other ways, the Spirit of the Risen Lord reveals the will of God for salvation and service. Who does not rejoice that the scepter is in the hands that were pierced for our sins, and that the power rests with the One whose heart was broken for us on Calvary? Such is the meaning of His divine Authority, when interpreted by Love.

Close akin is the message about "The Marching Orders of Our King."[5] The suggestion for the topic comes from the Duke of Wellington. When someone asked that gruff commander if he believed in Christian missions abroad, the Iron Duke replied, "Sir, what are your marching orders?" In a day when the gateways into distant lands have been clanging shut, and the gifts for the advancement of the Kingdom abroad have been declining, the

[4] Matt. 28:18; see D. W. Forrest, *The Authority of Christ,* T. & T. Clark, Edinburgh, 1908.

[5] Matt. 28:19-20.

local pastor should sound the call to make ready for an advance. Some of these times those gateways into the other half of the world will swing open wide. Let us make ready now to send forth groups of our strongest sons and daughters, that the kingdoms of this world may become the Kingdom of our Lord, and of His Christ.[6] Thus in world-wide missions may we find what William James used to style "the moral equivalent of war."

There may also be a sermon about "Putting on the Uniform of Christ."[7] The text refers to Christian baptism, which in terms of holy warfare means putting on the uniform of Christ as King, and enlisting in His service for life, both here and hereafter. "There is no discharge in that war."[8] Neither is there any desire to cease from following Him "whose service is perfect freedom." Such is the figure that one may use in presenting the facts about Christian baptism. At the heart of the whole matter is the need for personal loyalty to Christ as King.

Is it not time that many parts of the Church rediscover the glory of Christian baptism? Countless voices are recalling us to the old-time emphasis on the supremacy of the Lord's Supper. But a strong bishop in the Protestant Episcopal Church recently declared that in the New Testament there is even more about baptism than there is about the Eucharist. If that is correct, as it seems to be, there is a call for some kind of renaissance centering round the glory of the Triune God as revealed in the holy rite of baptism.

One of the most interesting current biographies is that of the late Walter Rauschenbusch.[9] When he was a little boy he attended church and Sunday school regularly, but all that he re-

[6] Rev. 11:15*b*.
[7] Matt. 28:19.
[8] Eccles. 8:8*c*.
[9] D. R. Sharpe, *Walter Rauschenbusch,* Macmillan, 1942, pp. 35, 153.

membered afterward was the baptisms and the communion services. In them he found an appeal to the imagination, a quality that was to help him gain distinction. In later years he attributed the habit of nonattendance among us Protestants to our individualism and our lack of emphasis on the Church. If his diagnosis was correct, we ought to make more of these two holy ordinances. We likewise need to do more of the "teaching" that our Master enjoins. Such is one purpose of the discourse now before us: "Baptize and teach!"

Another of these messages may be on "Christ, Our Contemporary." [10] This is the way the words run in the Greek: "Lo, I am with you all the days, even unto the end of the age." The promise is as up-to-date as the morning newspaper. Once when David Livingstone was in the heart of Africa, and was tempted to flee from the path of duty, he found solace in this text. "It is the word of a Gentleman of the most sacred and strictest honor, and there is an end on't." [11] Vital as it is to believe in "the Jesus of History" [12] and "the Christ of Prophecy," a man's religion calls even more insistently for loyalty to "the Christ of Today."

THE DEEPENING OF CHRISTIAN EXPERIENCE

When we turn to the latter part of St. John, we are in a different climate. The teachings here are still more deeply spiritual; they have to do with the inner meaning and glory of our religion. For instance, there may be a sermon about "The Christian Source of Peace." The text is brief and striking: "Peace be unto you." [13] What do we human beings need so

[10] Matt. 28:20b.

[11] W. G. Blaikie, *The Personal Life of David Livingstone*, Laymen's Missionary Movement, n.d., p. 197.

[12] Title of a good book by T. R. Glover, Doran, 1917.

[13] John 20:21b.

much today as inner peace? It comes through the presence of the Living Christ, who bestows the Holy Spirit upon us as soon as our hearts are open to receive Him by faith.

The following Sunday there may be a message on "The Conversion of an Honest Doubter."[14] The man in view is Thomas, who three times appears in this Gospel, and each time is expressing uncertainty about Christ. In a brief series, "A Strong Man's Doubts," there might be three sermons. If so, the emphasis each time ought to be on the way the Lord Jesus used the expression of doubt as a means of helping Thomas, as well as others. If ever a person needs a friend who is kind and patient, it is a young man trying to steer his boat through that fog known as doubt.

Doubt is mental uncertainty regarding some vital Christian truth. Speaking figuratively, doubt is a disorder of the soul. The underlying cause may or may not be sinful. In the experience of young Thomas there does not seem to have been any secret moral evil that led him to doubt. Rather was there a failure to see the light. Fortunately, he came to the One who alone is able to dispel every mist from the soul.[15]

Doubt is most likely to be prevalent among young people away at school. During their ministry at two educational centers the author and his wife discovered as much doubt among university girls as among the men. While some of those young folk would glibly quote the words of Robert Browning in "Rabbi Ben Ezra,"

> Rather I prize the doubt
> Low kinds exist without,
> Finished and finite clods, untroubled by a spark,

[14] John 20:28.
[15] See H. van Dyke, *The Gospel for an Age of Doubt*, Macmillan, 1896; P. C. Simpson, *The Fact of Christ*, Revell, 1901.

down in their hearts most of those victims were wretched. They wished that they might believe; they wanted to be sure about God. Each of them would have profited much from a personal conversation with a wise friend who could listen without being shocked. But most of them had to depend on such light as came from the pulpit.

Fortunately they seemed to welcome preaching that stressed the fact of the Living Christ. They were glad to learn about the transformation of an honest doubter into a triumphant witness. In the sermon, that is what one would stress. When Thomas became sure that he stood face to face with the Risen Lord, the young doubter exclaimed: "My Lord and my God!" Where, even in the New Testament, can one find a more ringing testimony to the Deity of our Lord? The value of the words appears from the fact that Christ welcomed such adoration.

THE TEACHING OF CHRISTIAN WORKERS

The twenty-first chapter of St. John is a sort of inspired postscript. It tells about the way in which the Risen Lord practically completed His "Training of the Twelve." [16] The opening paragraph suggests a sermon, "The Living Christ in Our Day's Work." [17] To the disciples, fishing on the Sea of Galilee was real labor; that was how most of them earned their daily bread. Into their midst as they toiled came the Lord Jesus. To this day He is concerned about men's work as well as their worship. He is with the sons of toil whenever they need counsel and strength. He knows; He cares; He is able to help. Especially does His heart go out to those who seem to have failed. Better still, the Living Christ is waiting to bless our work. If our efforts seem futile, He knows why, and He can

[16] Title of the classic work by A. B. Bruce, Armstrong and Son, 1902.
[17] John 21:6.

135

tell us what to do. "Cast the net on the right side of the ship, and ye shall find." The "right side" means the opposite of the left, but in another sense of the term, the Master's behest shows that He can point out the ideal place to catch fish. Strange as it may seem, He knows more about any kind of work than the most expert craftsmen ever dream of learning. Whatever a man's calling, the Lord Christ understands far more about it than the human workman can ever know.

The parallel with evangelistic activity is obvious. During the month of March, for example, at a typical meeting of an official board, under the leadership of a minister much like Peter, the lay officers reported that they had toiled all winter and taken nothing. Then they asked, "Under present conditions in our parish is it possible to have an ingathering of adult members on confession of faith?" To their inquiry the paragraph before us gives the inspired answer, for the passage is a sort of parable in action. It shows that the Living Christ is ready to bless those who labor to win souls under His guidance. "Launch out into the deep!"

The scene on the shore is another parable in action.[18] The Lord Jesus appears to have kindled the fire with His own hands. The paragraph as a whole makes clear that He continues to be with us after we have toiled and are ready for rest. Herein lies the secret of constant peace and joy: the Living Christ is with us when we worship, when we toil, and when we rest. Such is the meaning of the slogan "Fellowship and Service." This was the name of a Women's Bible Class which found in the Living Christ the inspiration for worship, Bible study, and Christian work. What an ideal!

In the passage before us the emphasis is on the group. Elsewhere in the Gospels religion usually concerns Christ and the

[18] John 21:9-13.

individual soul. But here and there are paragraphs that show the wisdom of having teamwork. In all things human there is need of organization, which should usually be simple and flexible. Before eleven men can work or worship together there must be some sort of leadership. If they are fishermen, they have need of a boat and a net, as well as experience in the craft. Most of all, such a group of Christians ought to be eager for the presence and blessing of the Living Christ. Whenever He is with His disciples, He should be in charge. Especially should the human leader, such as Simon Peter, defer to the will of the Divine Master and Friend.

The first part of this chapter also suggests a number of sermons about the disciples, notably Peter. One message would have to do with his unconscious influence. Among written sermons on that subject the present author remembers three, all of which had to do with Peter. The first discourse is the famous one by Horace Bushnell, "Unconscious Influence." [19] The second is by former Dean Charles R. Brown of Yale. The third was prepared by a first-year man in the Seminary. Needless to say, the three messages are alike only in the fact that each of them deals with unconscious influence.[20]

Why should three ministers, working independently, turn to the Apostle Peter as an object lesson of unconscious influence? Surely he was a man of the outgoing type, an extrovert. Except when the Lord Jesus was present, the personality of Peter appears to have dominated every group in which he moved. Nevertheless, even in the case of such a masterful man as Simon Peter, his unconscious influence seems to have been mightier than what he did deliberately. Evidently the dynamic leader accomplishes most for his Master simply by being himself and

[19] *The New Life*, London, 1892, Sermon IX.
[20] The texts are John 20:8; John 21:3*a*; Acts 5:15.

going on in the path of duty. Peter was most useful and influential when he forgot about himself and simply did what he knew to be the will of God. On the human level, therefore, the chief essential in a church leader is a personality like that of the Lord Jesus.

Another suggestion has to do with the fire of coals.[21] Once before, in the Judgment Hall, Simon Peter stood at a fire and warmed himself. There he denied that he so much as knew the Lord Jesus. Now the penitent disciple is standing at another fire and listening eagerly to this same Christ. The contrast is between finding fellowship with the children of the world and with the friends of the Lord Jesus. In each of the two scenes there is an appeal to the eye of the soul. In the resulting sermon one should lead the hearer to ask, "At whose fire am I seeking my fellowship, at that of the world or at this of my Lord?"

The next paragraph may lead to a sermon about "The Meaning of Religion as Love." [22] "Lovest thou me more than these?" The question of our Lord, repeated twice for emphasis, shows that a man's religion is a matter of personal loyalty to Jesus Christ. Prior to his experience at the Cross Peter had boasted that he alone would be true to the Master. Now the chastened disciple is humbly professing his allegiance to this same Living Christ. The Lord Jesus accepts him once again and bids him show his loyalty by service as a shepherd.[23]

THE ACCESS OF SPIRITUAL POWER

Now we turn to the opening chapter of Acts, for the most

[21] John 21:9.

[22] John 21:15-19. In Greek exegesis there are two interesting questions: one relates to the pronoun "these," the other to the verbs translated "love." The writer believes that the pronoun refers to the disciples: "Lovest thou me more than these others love me?" and that the verbs are practically interchangeable, as in John 11:3, 5 (Greek). Such matters, however, have no place in the pulpit.

[23] Cf. I Pet. 5:1-4.

difficult of all these sermons, the one about the Ascension.[24] Nonetheless, if a man perseveres in study until he is ready to preach, he will find the quest rewarding. So will the people be grateful for light upon what has hitherto seemed to be only a Biblical puzzle. Amidst all the mysteries that cluster around the Ascension, two facts shine out clearly. The one has to do with earth, the other with heaven. Both concern power, the keynote of Acts.

First of all, the Ascension marked the close of our Lord's life on earth. From a certain point of view the drama of our redemption started with Christmas Day, went on past Calvary to the Resurrection, and from the Ascension to the Day of Pentecost. In this fivefold succession, which involves the major events of the Christian Year, there could have been no Calvary and no Resurrection without a preceding Incarnation, and there could have been no Pentecost without a prior Ascension.

In the days of His flesh our Lord chose to be in only one place at a time, but now by His Spirit He is with the children of God everywhere. Surely it is better by far to have Him with us here, and with His loved ones everywhere, than if we could be with Him only by making a journey to the Holy Land. It is no wonder, then, that some of us do not care to have our little ones sing plaintively:

> I think when I read that sweet story of old,
>> When Jesus was here among men,
> How He called little children as lambs to His fold,
>> I should like to have been with them then.

On the other hand, the Ascension marked the beginning of Christ's heavenly reign. Not only is He everywhere; He wields

[24] Acts 1:9-11; cf. Heb. 4:14-16. See William Milligan, *The Ascension and Heavenly Priesthood of Our Lord*, London, 1894; J. S. Stewart, *The Strong Name* (sermons), Scribner, 1941, pp. 46-57.

all the powers of the Godhead. At the Ascension He assumed all the glories that He had laid aside at the Incarnation. Although these truths are veiled in mystery, it is a mystery of light, not of darkness. Shining out through the mists that cluster around the Ascension is the clear truth that He who once was the lowly Nazarene is now exalted as Lord of heaven and earth. That is why we say in the Apostles' Creed: "He ascended into heaven, and sitteth at the right hand of God the Father Almighty." Is it any wonder that this truth led Handel to compose the "Hallelujah Chorus" as the climax of *The Messiah*? "King of Kings, and Lord of Lords, Hallelujah!"

The last of these messages, the one about Pentecost, should be the best. The subject ought to be something about the Holy Spirit, perhaps as "The Power of God in the Lives of Men." [25] The Spirit is more than Power; He is also Wisdom and Beauty; in fact, He is the Personal Representative of God. But in preaching to matter-of-fact Americans it may be wise to stress the Holy Spirit as power. What else does the average man desire so much? He longs for power to know the truth, to do the right, and to become a better person.

For such a gift of the gods many a modern man would give almost anything short of life itself. In fact, Thomas H. Huxley once declared that for such mastery over self and things he would gladly forfeit his freedom as a man: "I protest that if some great Power would agree to make me always think what is true and do what is right, on condition of being turned into a sort of clock and wound up every morning before I get out of bed, I should instantly close with the offer." [26] Alas, Professor Huxley, you seem never to have found the Source of such spiritual might! The gift is free for the redeemed children of God.

[25] Acts 2:2-3.
[26] *Lay Sermons, Addresses, and Reviews* Appleton, 1871, p. 340.

On what terms then does the Risen Lord bestow the power of the Spirit? In the case before, and doubtless in every other, the conditions are three. First, the Holy Spirit is promised to believers in Christ. Again, the Spirit is given in answer to united prayer. Still further, His power is available for Christian service, especially in the form of witnessing for Christ. Such a Christian worker as Dwight L. Moody or Mary Slessor of Calabar found available all the spiritual power needed for any task in hand. In return for infilling with strength from on high, each of them gave the glory to God.

One Sunday night years ago when Oscar F. Blackwelder of Washington, D. C., was a student in the seminary, he listened to a sermon about Pentecost. Since the subject was "An Old-Fashioned Revival," the man in the pulpit made free use of old-time alliteration. His emphasis was on the fact that we Christians today can have such a spiritual quickening in the local church on much the same conditions as at Pentecost. That old-fashioned revival was—

> Preceded by Old-Fashioned Prayer,
> Accomplished by Old-Fashioned Preaching,
> Followed by Old-Fashioned Piety.

Twenty years later the two ministers had an opportunity to become well acquainted. The younger man was somewhat amazed to find that the other had no recollection of that sermon. Even when he heard about it he did not recognize the trail as familiar. Such an experience shows once again that God's Word has a way of impressing itself on the heart of the hearer. It does not return unto God void, but rather serves as the seed-corn of the Kingdom that is to come on earth. Should not every minister, therefore, preach often concerning the Holy Spirit as the Power of God in the lives of men?

Chapter VIII

PREACHING BIBLE ETHICS

IN THE AFTERGLOW OF EASTER THERE IS A CALL FOR EMPHASIS ON
Biblical ethics. The new converts should learn how to live
among men according to the will of God, and the members of
longer standing need to be taught the meaning of Christian duty.
Such preaching is doubly necessary in a day when the world is
at war, or in a time of ensuing reconstruction.

Before Easter the stress is on doctrine; afterwards, on ethics.
Both are vital, but the doctrine should come first, for it is the
basis of the duty. Such a succession is in harmony with the
Bible as a whole. According to the Westminster Shorter Catechism, "The Scriptures principally teach what man is to believe
concerning God, and what duty God requires of man." While
it is impossible to measure such things accurately, the Bible
probably contains as much about ethics as about doctrine.

What, then, is an ethical sermon? It is the preacher's interpretation of a Christian duty, for a practical purpose. The desire
is to present clearly and strongly a certain duty, such as the forgiveness of wrongs. The purpose is to guide the hearer in living
according to the will of God as revealed in a certain passage.
The sermon, however, should be an exposition of the duty, and
not merely an interpretation of the passage, for the aim is practical. Such preaching may come at the second service on Sunday.

The emphasis should be largely on the individual, since the
desire is to deal with the difficulties of the Christian soul. It
would be possible to discuss the moral problems of the world
at large, but that kind of pulpit work is most exacting. It calls

PREACHING BIBLE ETHICS

for the wisdom and breadth of a theologian and saint. Without being cowardly, the parish minister can leave to spiritual statesmen such ambitious discourses, while he gives himself to the moral problems of the man in the pew. Of course some of them relate to world peace, universal brotherhood, and the removal of race prejudice. Even so, the sermon ought to bring the Biblical teaching home to the conscience of the lay hearer. At the end of the hour he should say, "Lord, what wilt Thou have me to do?"

Such pulpit work appeals to the conscience. In fact, one ought to preach at times directly on that subject. Fortunately, the Bible is full of materials for case studies in the workings of a man's conscience. Both in the Old Testament and in the New there is more about the matter than in the writings of George Eliot and Hawthorne, Shakespeare and Ibsen, not to mention the Greek tragedians and the Russian novelists. Here are the topics of a brief series, under the heading, "What the Bible Says About Conscience."

The Bible a Book of Conscience...............II Tim. 3:16
The Christian Standard of Conscience.............Matt. 5:48
The Lord of the Christian Conscience...........Matt. 7:28-29
The Secret of a Healthy Conscience................Acts 24:16
The Everyday Workings of Conscience...........I Cor. 10:31
The Cleansing of a Man's Conscience...............Heb. 9:14

THE TEN COMMANDMENTS

Another fertile field for ethical preaching is the Ten Commandments. Instead of lumping them all up in a single sermon or two, why not have a course or a series? In either case the introductory sermon may be from the Preface.[1] The resulting message ought to give a popular bird's-eye view of the Ten

[1] Exod. 20:2.

143

Words. There need be only two broad lines of thought: the first has to do with man's duty to God; the second, with man's duty to man. Thus the two parts of the sermon correspond with the First Table of the Law and the Second.[2]

Any such message ought to come in the midst of uplifting worship. The hymns and the prayers should have to do with human needs other than those in the sermon. Just before the pastor speaks, there may be an inspiring hymn, such as "How firm a foundation." While the people are still standing, they should repeat in unison with the minister the Ten Commandments. Then he should utter the saying of our Lord, who interprets the Law in terms of love.[3]

Of the two Tables, the First is the more important. It is basic; that may be why it stands first. Man's duty to man rests upon man's duty to God. The person who gets right with God, and keeps close to Him in love and faith, should have no insuperable difficulty in doing his duty towards his neighbor.

In the First Table the most vital commandment is the one at the beginning. This Word is also the most difficult to interpret and obey, since it calls for "The God-Centered Life": "Thou shalt have no other gods before me." "To have God," says Martin Luther, "is to trust Him." "Before me" is in His presence, and He is everywhere. To have no other gods before Him means to recognize only one God on earth and in heaven. He is the One whom we know in Christ Jesus. The First Commandment is missionary. In modern terms, it means, "Thou shalt make thy world Christian." Even today, thousands of years after the time of Moses, scarcely a third of the human race professes to "have" the one true God, and many of those who

[2] For various ways of dividing the two Tables, see Charles Hodge, *Systematic Theology,* Scribner, 1893, III, 272-75.

[3] Matt. 22:37-40.

make the profession with their lips belie it in their lives. When shall we mortals begin to put God first in all that we say and do?

The Second Commandment, also, is missionary; it calls for "Spiritual Worship." There is to be no adoration of the true God by means of images, or of false gods by the use of idols. There should be no idolatry among the millions of India, and no image-worship among the peoples of Latin America. While the vast majority of the earth's inhabitants are nominally religious, not one person in four attempts to keep the Second Commandment. In recent years our eyes are turning more and more to the countries south of our own. In that "other America" much of the religion, so called, has come down from paganism and has scarcely been altered by baptism in the name of the Christian God. Consequently university graduates in Argentina, Peru, and other lands to the South have been alienated from the Church. But why should we look beyond our own borders? Is there not a vast deal of image-worship and idolatry here at home? We all need the Living God.

The Third Commandment calls for "Reverence in Speech." The injunction is timely, for in places high and low, profanity and other forms of vulgar speech abound. On the stage the use of oaths is a matter of course; among novels few of the best-sellers are free from the blight; in conversation it is common for even professing Christians to take the name of the Lord in vain. As a rule the cause is thoughtlessness. But if a gentleman never "lightly and unadvisedly" uses the name of his wife or mother, should he not also revere the name of his God? Especially in days of war and reconstruction there is likely to be an increase of profanity. When hosts of men live together, far from the restraints of home and mother, freedom of speech often leads to license. And yet the books about the Ten Commandments say that profanity is passing out of vogue! [4] Perhaps this mistaken notion accounts for the fact that the books usually discuss something other than the direct teaching of the Third Commandment.

There is likewise need of emphasis on the Fourth Word, which calls for "The Day of Rest and Worship." That means setting apart one day in seven for bodily relaxation and spiritual uplift. To rest is not to rust. Instead of idleness and stagnation there should be a complete change of thought and activity. For the present-day man or woman the best way to relax is to worship God in the sanctuary. There is also a place for household joys. The Fourth Commandment is social as well as religious. Really there is no great gulf fixed between social ethics and religious truth, but we can think of them separately. In Exodus the reason annexed to the Fourth Word has to do with God's creation of the world; [5] in Deuteronomy the parallel passage concerns a man's duty to his neighbor.

The person who keeps the Lord's Day because of loyalty to God will make it possible for his neighbor to enjoy a weekly day of rest and worship. While we Christians set apart the first day of the week, and not the Jewish Sabbath, human needs are much the same now as in the time of Moses. For a day to be holy means that it should be different, and far better than other days. According to the Bible, the day of rest and worship ought to be like heaven. In view of conditions everywhere at present, however, it is a question whether or not we have a day that is worthy of being handed down to coming generations. As soon as there is in our land a revival of religion,

[4] See H. S. Coffin, *The Ten Commandments,* Doran, 1915, p. 58; R. W. Dale, *The Ten Commandments,* Hodder & Stoughton, London, n.d., p. 71. Another suggestive book is J. O. Dykes, *The Law of the Ten Words,* Doran, n.d.
[5] Exod. 20:8-11; cf. Deut. 5:12-15.

one of the marks will be a more widespread observance of the Lord's Day.

Thus far we have thought about five sermons, one concerning the Preface and four about the parts of the First Table. This is material enough for a brief series, of which the subject may be, "The Basis of the Ten Commandments." After a rest for a few weeks the congregation should welcome a discussion of the Second Table, under the heading, "The Human Side of God's Law."

Once again, the most vital commandment heads the list: "Honor thy father and thy mother." The ideal here is "Loyalty to Parents," for the most important fact about any home is loyalty. The child should be faithful to his father, for the worthy father is much like God; so is the good mother. The injunction to honor each of them applies to the babe when he first responds to his mother's smile, to the growing lad as he learns to swim in deepening waters, and to the full-grown man whose father and mother are aged. In fact, they may no longer be in the flesh. The best way to honor any godly parent is to become the same kind of Christian.

In the Fifth Word the reference is to both parents, especially the father. In our homeland there is need of such counsel. In other countries, such as parts of Africa, man looks down on woman, but with us the tendency is to make light of the husband and father. After lauding mother to the skies, as though she were almost divine, our best-known evangelist used to say, "Any old stick is good enough to be a dad!" Of course the speaker was trying to be facetious, but what right has a minister of the Gospel to crack cheap jokes about the person who ought to be like God the Father Almighty?

The Sixth Commandment is made out of still sterner stuff: "Thou shalt not kill." The ideal here is "The Sanctity of Human

Life." There is a direct prohibition of murder, and there is a bearing on the sin of war. Of all the collective evils on earth, war is doubtless the worst. It brings in its train everything else that is vile, from famine and pestilence to moral filth and spiritual apostasy. Instead of teaching young men to regard human life as the gift of God, and the human body as the temple of the Holy Spirit, war encourages them to think of life as cheap and of the body as cannon fodder.

There is also a bearing on such social sins as reckless driving on the highways. In the United States each year irresponsible automobilists have been causing greater loss of life than we suffered among our soldiers and sailors in camp and on the field during any twelve months of the first World War. The slaughter on our highways has been due largely to the use of liquor. Nevertheless, our government is encouraging drivers to buy and drink whiskey. Almost every highway is lined with signs suggesting that the driver stop and imbibe what may bring death to himself and others. Places for the sale of liquor have seemed almost as frequent as the signs. In view of these facts, is the Christian pulpit to hold its peace? If so, let the preacher consider the words of the prophet: "We have made a covenant with death, and with hell are we at agreement." [6] The prophetic words have to do directly with strong drink. Especially in a day of world-wide war many of us wish that there were no such evil as the sale of intoxicating liquor.

The teaching of the Sixth Commandment is that every life comes as the gift of infinite love. If so, is it ever a Christian man's duty to engage in war? Opinions differ sharply. With all regard for holy men who think otherwise, the author believes that a purely defensive war is sometimes a tragic necessity. Surely Abraham did the will of God when he hurried forth with

[6] Isa. 28:15a.

148

his armed troops and rescued captured Lot.[7] If the uncle had not gone to war, he would have sinned against God. If the United States had not gone to war of late, what would be the hope for the world of tomorrow? Where would be the field for missions and for the Protestant Church?

In one of the best of current novels [8] a moving scene has to do with the problem of war in an acute form. The hero, Father Chisholm, a Roman Catholic priest in China, has been a pronounced pacifist. But when the local leader of the bandit forces demands the delivery of the native women and children, as well as the men, to a fate far worse than death, the clergyman enters the conflict and wins the day. Who will dare to claim that such an act was wrong? If he had done nothing, how could he ever have lived with his conscience? But still the decision to take up arms against his fellow men caused Father Chisholm untold anguish. When he explained to his Chinese comrade the plan for destroying the machine-gun nest of the brigand forces, the other man replied, "My friend, I must continue to regard you as a gift from heaven." Then the padre said, with a sigh, "I have forgotten about heaven tonight." Alas, war is like hell, not heaven!

The Seventh Word is still harder to discuss in public, since this Word calls for "The Preservation of Purity," or "Purity Between the Sexes." Everywhere today such teaching is imperative. In some of its sectors the first World War was a training school in sexual sin. The Administration, however, took a determined stand against the indulgence in sexual sin by any soldier or sailor. In many training camps during the second World War conditions have been still more deplorable, and those in control seem to be powerless.

[7] Gen. 14.
[8] A. J. Cronin, *The Keys of the Kingdom*, Little, Brown, 1940, pp. 263-71.

Let us come closer home. In the average community our boasted systems of sex instruction have broken down. In some high schools immorality is rife. If a full-blooded young fellow is to keep himself unspotted from the world, something more is needful than scientific instruction about the meaning of sex. Now that contraceptives are on sale openly in almost every drugstore, many a growing girl deems it safe to sin with her body. But what about the blot on her soul?

In preaching through the Ten Commandments, therefore, be sure to stress the Seventh. Do not apologize for being frank. What every young person needs today, as in the time of Joseph, is faith in the Living God: "How then can I do this great wickedness, and sin against God?" [9] Apart from the Christian home, the best place to give ethical teaching is at the local church. Without being prudish or suggestive, the pastor can hold up the Biblical ideal. It is that every man or boy should look on every woman or girl as a person, not a thing. Even if she is not yet so pure as she ought to be, he can encourage her to become a daughter of the King.

Such an ideal calls for the dedication of the body to the Lord from whom it came. Every man's body should be a temple for the indwelling of the Holy Spirit; every girl's body should be a shrine where purity and honor make their home. According to a well-known clergyman, a man looks on his body in one of three ways. The Christian says to his Lord: "My body for Thee." The worldling says to his mirror: "My body for myself." The wicked man says to a woman: "Thy body for me." Is there no need of a sermon on "Religion for a Man's Body"? [10]

The Eighth Commandment concerns "The Private Ownership of Property." The Scriptures recognize a man's God-given right

[9] Gen. 39:9c; cf. Otto Piper, *The Christian Interpretation of Sex,* Scribner, 1941.
[10] See I Cor. 6:13b; I Cor. 6:19-20; Rom. 12:1.

to possess things. In the ideal world there is to be no social injustice. In the golden age of which the prophets sing, the farmer is to own the place where he dwells.[11] The promise relates to the time when religion will prevail on earth, and when the laws of the nations will be righteous. Then there will be no more war.

Meanwhile there is need of pulpit instruction based on the text: "Thou shalt not steal." It is easy to inveigh against the sins of distant capitalists. Such invectives are as cheap as they are ineffective. Only in an exceptional parish does a godless plutocrat help to pay the coal bills. Rather does the friend in the pew need a clear, kind, practical interpertation of what honesty requires from him today. Without telling a man how to run his business, or how to be a better salesman, the pastor can encourage him to live and work as a Christian in the midst of an ungodly world. Even a few laymen of the right sort can help to lift the moral standards of the entire community.

The Eighth Word has to do indirectly with gambling, a subject to which one should devote at least a part of a sermon. According to Herbert Spencer, in gambling

pleasure is obtained at the cost of pain to another. The normal obtainment of gratification, or of the money which purchases gratification, implies, firstly, that there has been put forth equivalent effort of the kind which in some way furthers the general good; and implies, secondly, that those from whom the money is received get directly or indirectly equivalent satisfactions. But in gambling the opposite happens. Benefit received does not imply effort put forth; and the happiness of the winner involves the misery of the loser. This kind of action is therefore antisocial—sears the sympathies, cultivates a hard egoism, and so produces a general deterioration of character and conduct.[12]

[11] Mic. 4:4.
[12] *The Study of Sociology,* Appleton, 1874, p. 306.

Equally exacting is the next commandment. The Ninth Word enjoins "The Sanctity of the Truth": "Thou shalt not bear false witness against thy neighbour." This statute has to do with slander as well as perjury. The commandment likewise forbids gossip and other forms of lying. The Biblical ideal here, as elsewhere, is a lofty regard for the truth, whatever the cost to the teller. The Lord God calls on everyone to protect his neighbor's reputation. If once a man forfeits that, even through no fault of his own, he is of all men the most pitiable. As for a woman, when once her fair name is gone, there is no hope, except in God.

Nevertheless, the meanest scoundrel in town can throw mud and slime on the garments of the purest saint. In the days of His flesh even our Lord did not escape being regarded as a moral leper. When shall we ministers learn to stress the importance of reputation?

> Good name in man or woman, dear my lord,
> Is the immediate jewel of their souls:
> Who steals my purse steals trash; 'tis something, nothing;
> 'Twas mine, 'tis his, and has been slave to thousands;
> But he that filches from me my good name
> Robs me of that which not enriches him
> And makes me poor indeed.[13]

The Tenth Commandment is comparatively easy to discuss in a sermon. This Word appears last because it is climactic; apart from the Fifth Commandment, it is the most important part of the Second Table. It warns against "The Sin of Covetousness." The contrasting virtue is contentment. Just as covetousness is the root of many other sins, so is contentment the wellspring of countless blessings.

[13] Shakespeare *Othello*, III, 3, 155-61.

The teaching concerns a man's relation to money. At the Day of Judgment, according to the late Bishop Charles H. Fowler, more men will be condemned because of sinful attitudes towards money than for all other reasons combined. Doubtless the statement is extreme; at least it is incapable of proof. But the tenor is in accord with the warnings of the prophets and the apostles, as well as the Master. The Biblical teachings set before the minister the example of preaching boldly about money.

When regarded as an end in itself, and not as a means of doing good, money is a peril. But when employed in building up the Kingdom of God through the home and the church, money may be a means of grace. Since these matters bulk large in the Bible, and in the experience of men today, there should be a good deal of pastoral instruction about the Christian use of money. No sort of preaching is more timely and interesting.

Sermons about the Commandments, one by one, should lead up to a message about them as a whole. The point of view should be that of our Lord,[14] who accepted this Law at its face value and interpreted it all in the light of His love. In summing up the Law, He said that the Christian should love God supremely, love his neighbor largely, and love himself last. Nowhere else can one find a more accurate description of what it means to be a disciple. In fact, these words provide a cameo of the Lord Jesus.

"Thou shalt love thy neighbor as thyself." Your neighbor is the man who needs you, whether he lives across the street or beyond the sea. Thus far there is clear sailing, but what does one learn from the phrase "as thyself"? It shows that while love for God is first, and love for neighbor is second, love for oneself also has a place. Not in the way of selfishness, but through a desire to serve, the Christian should make the most of all his God-

[14] Matt. 22:37-40.

153

given powers and graces. While it is not a man's first duty, or even his second, self-improvement is no small part of his religion and life here below.

Herein lies the basis of education, athletics, and other ways of developing a man's personality. On the other hand, when a young fellow is morally wild, we say that he is "letting himself go." When a woman neglects her appearance she is "not taking care of herself." When a man drinks to excess he does not love himself enough to keep sober. When a girl goes wrong she does not love herself sufficiently to keep her soul unspotted.

Thus the series about "The Human Side of God's Law" may include seven sermons. This number includes one concerning each Word in the Second Table, and a closing message about the Ten Commandments as interpreted by the Lord of Love.

If any minister is asking, "What shall I do on Sunday evenings after Easter?" let him seriously consider preaching about the Ten Commandments. Especially in dealing with the Second Table he will be presenting subjects of vital concern to every man or woman. But before the pastor embarks on either series he ought to make a careful study of the Decalogue as a whole. If he does that with care he may have at home the equivalent of a postgraduate course in Biblical ethics.[15]

The sermons might have a place in the evangelistic program for the year. If so, they would come earlier in the season, perhaps in the autumn. In the South, one of the most effective soul-winning pastors reports that his most gratifying ingathering came as a consequence of a course based on the Ten Commandments. The messages followed one after another, all at the morning service. While each discourse was in keeping with its Biblical

---

[15] See John Drewett, *The Ten Commandments in the Twentieth Century*, S.P.C.K., London, 1941; C. G. Chappell, *Ten Rules for Living* (sermons), Abingdon-Cokesbury, 1938; R. H. Charles, *The Decalogue*, Edinburgh, 1923.

basis, the minister was much more intent on present-day values than on scholastic interpretation. In sermon after sermon he used the Law of God to show the layman his need of Christ and the Cross.

Such preaching is masculine, and it appeals to the best that is in the hearer. Today, as of old, the Law is the servant of God to show a man his need of the Saviour. At Wooster College, in Ohio, when the late President Lewis E. Holden was a senior there, one of his classmates expressed a desire to become a Christian, but protested that he felt no sense of sin and no need of the Saviour. Young Holden advised him: "Go to your room; lock your door; get down on your knees; and read the Ten Commandments. Then see what happens."

A little later the young fellow came bounding into Holden's room, exclaiming: "It worked! Before I had finished reading the First Commandment I saw that I am a sinner and that I need the Saviour." In later years that man became a prominent minister in the Baptist Church. Dearly did he love to preach both the Law and the Gospel, especially the latter. Much of his power as a winner of souls may have been due to his personal experience in discovering the Christ of the Cross by reading the Ten Commandments in the spirit of prayer.

THE SERMON ON THE MOUNT

In the New Testament, also, there is a good deal of ethical teaching, which has more to do with the individual than with society. For instruction about the wider circles of human duty one can turn to the Old Testament, notably to such a prophet as Amos or Isaiah. But for teachings concerning one's duty toward a fellow man, one need only listen to the sayings of our Lord. The Sermon on the Mount, so called, is really "The Teaching on the Hill." While the Lord Jesus may have uttered these words at different times and places, there is a certain advantage in thinking about them as the report of what He said at a summer Bible conference.

When one starts to prepare a number of popular messages about "The Teaching on the Hill," one finds it hard to keep the number of addresses within reasonable limits, since every paragraph contains the seed-thoughts for helpful messages. While the discussion below concerns nine sermons, it would be better to have only six, or not more than eight. The idea is to be suggestive, not exhaustive. The general subject may be "The Sermon on the Mount for Today," and the introductory discourse may be about "The Religion of the Modern Man." [16]

Many a man on the street has been saying, "I get my religion from the Sermon on the Mount." With some such starting point one can show that "The Teaching on the Hill" is for professing Christians, and that the Lord Jesus is telling His personal followers about the meaning of God's Kingdom. The first main part of His teaching has to do with the citizens of the Kingdom, who are spiritual.[17] They are like the Lord Jesus, and He is like God. The central portion of His instruction here is about the standards of the Kingdom, which are much more exacting than many of us think.[18] The closing section is about the ideals of Christian men, ideals that are loftier by far than in any other religion on earth.[19]

The purpose of this introductory message is not to explain "The Teaching on the Hill" so much as to guide the layman in reading it for himself at home. From this same practical viewpoint the next discourse may be about "The Portrait of the Chris-

[16] Matt. 5:1-2.
[17] Matt. 5:3-16.
[18] Matt. 5:17–6:18.
[19] Matt. 6:19–7:27.

tian," to be found in the Beatitudes.[20] In preaching on them be sure to show that they are spiritual, for they assume that the follower of our Lord is honest and brave; they insist that he also be humble and kind. Thus they afford a fairly accurate word painting of the Master Himself.

The following sermon may be on "The Two Ways of Doing Good." [21] Both the salt and the light are symbols: the one tells of the influence that is invisible and unconscious; the other speaks of what everyone can see clearly if he so desires. Thus we have the sort of basic contrast that should lead to an absorbing message. Is a man's religion a matter of unconscious influence, or of doing good in the open? It is both: from the life of many a believer goes forth the silent, pervasive influence that few of his neighbors appreciate, because it is as silent as the working of the salt; at the same time there is the doing of good deeds that everyone can behold. Meanwhile, the question is how to keep the balance.

Once a friend asked Harry Lauder, the Scotch comedian, what he undertsood by being a Christian in business. His answer was in terms of the old lamplighter in the village where Harry had lived as a boy. In the evening after his day of toil down in the mine the lad would watch his elderly friend come along the street and light every lamp in its turn. As soon as he had completed his rounds, he would go to his home and then to bed. While he slept, amid the darkness and sometimes the storm, those lights would lead many a belated pilgrim safe to his destination. In like manner, said Harry Lauder, the Christian should start burning for God many lives that will be a means of blessing long after the lamplighter himself has fallen asleep.

The sermon following may be on "The Passing Grade in

[20] Matt. 5:3-12.
[21] Matt. 5:13-16.

Christ's School." [22]   In appraising an institution of learning one asks first about the standards for admission and graduation. The more they are exacting, the more does a man admire that school. In the one now before us the passing grade is a hundred per cent; for to be perfect as our Heavenly Father is perfect means to live without sin, and to possess every virture in its fullness. Obviously that is impossible; and yet many a worldly man boasts that he lives according to the Sermon on the Mount, whereas the dear fellow has not as yet enrolled in the Lord's kindergarten. However, to tell him that might not be wise.

Fortunately, Christ Jesus makes possible whatever He requires. Not only is He our Teacher, whose standards are as high as heaven; He is also our Divine Friend, whose mercies never fail; He is likewise our Saviour, whose Cross is ever near. If any sinful mortal opens his eyes to see the ethical standards of the Sermon on the Mount, he should feel impelled to fall down at the foot of the Cross and ask for pardon and cleansing. Thus once again the teaching of ethics from the pulpit should lead to the conversion of the unsaved man in the pew, who needs to quit trusting in himself and begin relying on God.

A week later one may preach on "The Forgiveness of Wrongs." [23]   No other subject, unless it be money, bulks so large in our Lord's teachings about the Kingdom. In the sermon one should somehow make clear what one means by a wrong: it is a serious injury, or offense, committed by one mortal against another. Of course there may be a million on either side, as in a war, but it is easier to think of a single wrongdoer and a single victim, as representative of many. Whatever the number of persons involved, the offense in view is serious. As for the pinpricks that annoy a man from day to day, the only

[22] Matt. 5:48.
[23] Matt. 6:14-15.

thing to do with them is to ignore and forget, but a grievous wrong calls for serious treatment.

What, then, does the forgiveness of wrongs mean on the part of the man who is the innocent victim? The teachings of our Lord, here and elsewhere, are plain: a man's forgiveness of wrongs ought to be like God's forgiveness of sins. That is full; it is free; it is forever. In bringing about the reconciliation with the one who has done him the deadly wrong, the child of God takes the first step, and all the other measures he can, until he wins the wrongdoer. Thus it was with Joseph in his dealings with the brothers who had sold him into slavery.[24]

"But how is it possible for a human being to forgive? To err is human, but to forgive is divine! Is not that the most Godlike truth about God?" Yea, verily; but still our Lord again and again teaches that without forgiveness of wrongs there can be no religion in a man's soul. Fortunately, what He requires He makes possible through prayer, for it is no accident that most of our Lord's teachings about forgiveness of offenses are in connection with prayer. When Stephen was dying, that first Christian martyr prayed, "Lord, lay not this sin to their charge."[25] Doubtless he knew that on the Cross our Lord "prayed for them that did the wrong." In the awful days of war and its aftermath what do we mortals need more than the spirit that can say, "Father, forgive them; for they know not what they do"?[26]

Another timely subject that bulks large in the records of our Lord's teaching is a man's attitude toward money. In the text before us now the Master is telling about "The Treasures of the Heart."[27] What He enjoins is twofold: it concerns the folly

[24] Gen. 45:5-8; 50:19-21.
[25] Acts 7:60*a*.
[26] Luke 23:34*a*.
[27] Matt. 6:19-20.

of setting one's heart upon things that do not endure, and the wisdom of living for treasures that are eternal. Elsewhere in His popular teachings our Lord usually puts the light before the darkness, or the good before the bad. But here he starts with the folly of covetousness, over against the virtue of contentment. Homiletically, the rule is to put in the forefront what you wish the hearer to remember most clearly.[28]

Why is it foolish to set one's heart on things? The reference here is to food, clothing, shelter, and other personal property that a man really needs. The sin lies in making them the ends of existence here below, and not the means for doing the will of God. The folly appears from the fact that if a man lives for things he may get them or he may not; if he gets them he may keep them or he may not; if he keeps them they may become a curse to him and his household. In any case, if they do not leave him, erelong he must leave them. Is it not true in every man's experience, as well as among his circle of friends, that worldly possessions are more likely to be weights than wings?

On the other hand, think of the person who lays up treasure in heaven. Like Henry Drummond and Sir Wilfred Grenfell, or Alice Freeman Palmer and Mary Slessor, the person now in view lives for people because of love for God. The child of God is glad to invest time and strength, as well as substance, in the upbuilding of people, especially young folk and children. These friends for whom the Christian employs things as means of blessing are going to live forever. So if any man is eager to lay up treasures in heaven while busily engaged with things on earth, let him become a trustee of God's property, and use it all for the welfare of His children here below.

Once when Bishop Edwin H. Hughes was a young pastor

[28] See H. L. Hollingworth, *The Psychology of the Audience*, American Book Co., 1935, p. 98.

he spoke to a rural congregation about trusteeship for God. Afterward one of the most prosperous and influential farmers in the county took him home and entertained him at a sumptuous dinner. Seeing that his host had something to say in private, the minister suggested that the two of them take a walk. This is the substance of what the farmer said: "I began here without a penny, and I have earned everything that you see. I do not owe a mortal a dime, and I have money in the bank. In view of your sermon this morning, please tell me, if I do not own this farm, who does?" After a pause, during which he doubtless said a word of prayer, the young minister replied, "Mr. B., will you ask me that question a hundred years from today?"

The message following may be on "The Kingdom of God in Middletown Today," or else, "In Our Community." The text in view [29] is the key verse in the whole Gospel of Matthew, as well as in the Sermon on the Mount. To seek first the Kingdom means in part to do the will of God and likewise help others carry out His holy purposes. In short, put God first, others second, and self last. Then the promise is that the Heavenly Father will provide all the things a man needs with which to do His holy will. Such is the basic philosophy of the Christian life, here and hereafter.

To Madame Chiang Kai-shek, foremost Christian gentlewoman of our time,

religion means to try with all my soul and strength to do the will of God. Despondency and despair are no longer mine. . . . . Constantly exposed to danger, I am unafraid. I know that nothing on earth can happen to the General or to me until our work on earth is done.

In other words, the main product of a believer's life on earth is

[29] Matt.6:33.

spiritual. As for the by-products, they are material. Our Heavenly Father knows that we have need "of all these things" about which we worry and fret, but He wishes us to keep them in their proper place of God-given means for doing His will on earth as it is done in heaven.

Life is very simple [says this same leader among women], and yet how confused we make it seem. In old Chinese art there is in each picture only one outstanding object. Everything else is subordinated to that one beautiful thing. An integrated life is like that. What is the one beautiful flower? As I feel now, it is doing the will of God. I used to pray that God would do this or that. Now I pray only that God will make His will known to me.[30]

In the sermon about "The Meaning of the Golden Rule" [31] the appeal should be to the imagination. "Put yourself in the place of the other person. If you were where he is at present, how would you wish to be treated?" Here is an up-to-date version of the Golden Rule, as interpreted by love. This, then, is how every one of us should treat the Negro or the Japanese, the social outcast or the moral leper. Could any standard be loftier? In fact, unless a man's heart is full of love for Christ and for men, no one of us can begin to order his life in the spirit of the Golden Rule.

Toward the end of the series one can deal with "The House on the Rock." [32] Everyone likes to watch a new house going up, especially if it is to be his home. In these latter days many a thoughtful man has been asking anxiously about his life and work, "Will it last, or have I failed?" The answer depends large-

[30] *War Addresses and Other Selections*, China Information Committee, Hankow, 1938, p. 336.
[31] Matt. 7:12.
[32] Matt. 7:24-27.

ly on his choice of a foundation. Has he been building in accordance with the righteousness of God, or simply following the desires of his own heart? If a man builds for God, his work will be among "those things which cannot be shaken." [33]

> My hope is built on nothing less
> Than Jesus' blood and righteousness; . . . .
> On Christ, the solid rock, I stand;
> All other ground is sinking sand.

DEBATABLE ISSUES

Occasionally on a Sunday night it seems necessary to deal with some debatable issue of vital concern to the lay hearer. If so, it is good to find a text in one of the Epistles, including those by Paul, James, and Peter. Especially is First Corinthians rich in ethical values for it deals with the problem of how to be a Christian in the heart of a wealthy, wicked city. Amid such surroundings, instead of being a daily adventure of faith, a man's religion is more likely to become a struggle for survival. How, then, can he solve his moral problems, one by one?

The suggestion now is that one master First Corinthians as a whole and then be ready to preach from any relevant portion. Where else can one find more practical teachings about a man's duty to his fellow man? While the Epistle deals with each ethical problem in a different way, there is something of a basic pattern. It is this: in faith look upon every debatable issue from above, as it is in the eyes of God; in love approach the matter from within, as it concerns the brother in Christ; and in hope look forward to the ideal solution, as it will promote the cause

---

[33] Heb. 12:26-27—a strong preaching text. For a bibliography about the Sermon on the Mount, see D. A. Hayes, *The Heights of Christian Living,* Abingdon, 1929; also E. M. Ligon, *The Psychology of Christian Personality,* Macmillan, 1941.

of Christ and His Kingdom. Thus far the counsels are for the pastor in his study; now let us think about the moral problems of the layman.

For instance, there is the vexatious matter of questionable amusements, especially as they concern our young folk. About this whole subject there has been a vast deal of loose talking, some of it in the pulpit. Hence one should make it clear early in the discourse that certain things, such as honesty and helpfulness, are always and everywhere right, while other things, such as impurity and gambling, are never and nowhere pleasing to God. Between these two poles of right and wrong lie such matters as questionable amusements—for instance, going to see motion pictures. If we attend the right sort of performance, we do no wrong. If we remain at home, that is our privilege.

Thus far there seems to be clear sailing. Where, then, are the hidden rocks? Ofttimes they have to do with a weaker brother. For instance, there are local conditions that make it unwise for a minister to see pictures or play a game that would cause a brother to stumble. In Louisville, for example, only an occasional cleric or lay church officer would dare to attend the Derby, and yet everyone knows that horse racing may be an innocent sport. In any such debatable issue the deciding factor may be the welfare of one's weaker brother. This is the heart of the text in view: "If meat make my brother to offend, I will eat no flesh while the world standeth, lest I make my brother to offend." [34]

An ethical sermon is a sort of searchlight for the layman's soul. Partly for this reason the false prophet leaves such delicate issues severely alone. While he may be a kind of Biblical preacher, he never elects anything ethical. However, we need not think much about him, for he never reads this far in a book about a teach-

[34] I Cor. 8:13.

164

ing ministry. On the other hand, there is a fairly large school of devout believers who keep exhorting one another to eschew pulpit ethics, so as to preach the simple Gospel. To them in all kindness Phillips Brooks would say: "No powerful pulpit ever held aloof from the moral life of the community it lives in. . . . . When a strong, clear issue stands out plain, the preacher has his duty as sharply marked as that of the soldier on the field of battle." [85]

Once in a while local conditions call for a message that is certain to perplex some of these saints. They have so little tolerance for sexual sin that they think the subject should almost never emerge in the pulpit, at least not with reference to affairs in the home community today. They insist that the preacher should let them bask in the sunlight of God's grace, and rest on the promises of the Book. If he insists on inveighing against sin, let it be only in general, or else as it concerns the ancient Pharisees. If all this seems to be a caricature, the writer can take anyone to such a congregation not far away, and there point out some of the best Christians that he knows—except for this one blind spot. Even in the best of human beings every pastor learns to expect some sort of color blindness.

Here is a concrete case. During the first World War, in every community adjacent to a military encampment President Wilson and Secretary Baker caused the redlight district to be closed and kept under padlock. Several months after the signing of the Armistice, after all the troops had left a certain cantonment, the council of the city near by was asked to remove the legal ban against commercialized prostitution. On a certain Tuesday evening the matter was to come up for final decision. To one of the city pastors, and only one, the situation seemed to demand a special sermon, without any camouflage or smoke screen.

[85] *Lectures on Preaching,* Dutton, 1877, pp. 137, 142.

Through the newspapers he announced that on the Sunday evening prior to the meeting of the council he would preach on the topic, "Should Our City Legalize Sexual Sin?" How much his sermon had to do with the outcome he never tried to determine. As a rule, what such a situation needs most is exposure to the sunlight of popular opinion. At all events, when the council voted not to remove the padlocks from the local vestibules to the bottomless pit, that minister privately gave thanks to God.

Meanwhile, within part of the congregation there was a temporary tempest, for in that pulpit the traditions did not encourage the discussion of "political issues," a phrase that can be used to cover a multitude of sins. Following the announcement of the coming sermon, a few of the most regular churchgoers registered their protests in person. While others kept silent, they remained at home that night, or else attended where they could hear the Gospel. Nevertheless, the sanctuary was thronged, and everyone present learned, incidentally, about St. Augustine. In his *Confessions,* he writes feelingly about sexual sin, for in his early years he was a libertine. The pastor's text was one that Augustine long ago made famous: "Put ye on the Lord Jesus Christ, and make not provision for the flesh, to fulfil the lusts thereof." [36] The fact that the words are from Paul should have carried weight with the friends who felt that such preaching ought to be taboo. Those good folk looked up to Paul as a sort of Protestant pope. So do many of us regard him as the chief interpreter of Christian ethics, as well as Christian doctrine. In fact, his Epistles contain little else but doctrine and ethics, usually in this order.

On the morning after the sermon the pastor received through the mail an indignant missive, which had evidently been penned by a tremulous feminine hand. The sender was so shy that she

[36] Rom. 13:14.

did not even sign her name. This was what she wrote: "First Corinthians 2:2 is better than preaching about the redlight district." Yea, verily; but the gentle critic should have read on in that same Epistle. She would have found that in First Corinthians the Apostle says much about physical immorality as it slinks away from the sunlight of the Cross. If he were preaching in any such city today, how long would Paul keep silent in the face of a clear moral issue? Somehow or other, he always dealt with some life situation among the persons to whom he was speaking. Who follows in his train?

As for the anonymous letter, the pastor was tempted to make a heated reply from the pulpit. But ere he got his homiletical shotgun oiled and loaded, he laid the offending letter before the Lord. Perhaps for that reason his sense of humor asserted itself; so he burned the missive and hied forth to visit a parishioner who was ill. Since the city council took the action desired, he never again referred to the matter in public. Some years later, in looking back, he could see that the unsigned letter had done him good. So had the few others that came to the manse. For each of them he learned to give thanks, as for a thorn in the flesh.[37]

What should the pastor do with an unsigned letter that is critical or abusive? Let the answer come from John Kelman, a distinguished Scotch divine, who is addressing ministerial students at Yale:

If a man helps you to preach better, he has done you a benefit, even though in doing it he may have wounded you. Forget the personal affront to your infallibility, and judge the case as if it were the criticism of someone else's work. But whatever you do, never allow any critic to deflect your essential message, or to make you timid about letting the light of your vision shine. That is none of his business; it is God's and your own.[38]

[37] II Cor. 12:9-10.
[38] *The War and Preaching,* Yale University Press, 1919, p. 206.

KEEPING ONE'S BALANCE

In the preaching of Biblical ethics it is difficult to keep from swinging to one or the other of two extremes. The mature minister may close his eyes to things ethical and preach to ladies about "sweetness and light." An occasional excursion into the field of morals has taught him that a practical sermon about duty today is not acceptable to some of his dearest hearers. After an evening message about one of our Lord's many sayings concerning marriage and divorce, an elderly bachelor complained to the minister, "That sermon had no comfort for me!" Perhaps he would have been more concerned if he had been the father of four grown sons, with a number of grandchildren who were thinking of getting married.

On the other hand, the young clergyman may become so obsessed about reforming the world that he preaches little save ethics, and that rather stern. Most of his sermons may not be specially Biblical. Speaking on the basis of vast inexperience, with imperfect mastery of the Scriptures and other books, he may attempt to solve quickly and easily the most complicated problems of the nation and the world. In the seminary he should have learned that sound ethical preaching is the most difficult kind of pulpit work. While he is gradually getting his bearings, however, he will find that most of the members are patient with his sweeping generalizations. Even if the people do not learn much from him about the will of God for practical living today, at least they admire his enthusiasm and his courage.

Somewhere between the two extremes there is a pathway for every minister of the Gospel. One man may be specially qualified to interpret Christian ethics, whereas his neighbor is not, at least not yet. In one congregation there is more need of such work from the pulpit than in the adjoining parish. Herein may lie a reason for a change of pastorates after eight or ten years.

Since each minister tends to develop certain phases of the congregational life, and not others, normally there should be a number of good men who serve successively in the same field during any fifty years.

In the writer's experience as pastor, one church was well grounded in Biblical doctrine and not much concerned about Christian duty. In the next field the friends were eager to apply their religion, but they had hazy ideas about what they were supposed to apply. Consequently, the preaching program for one pulpit differed from the procedure in the other. In each case the purpose was to strengthen the weak part of the body. In football during spring practice the new coach sizes up his materials, and then during the summer he plans how to strengthen the weak spot at center, or in the backfield. So in the church the minister should ask the Holy Spirit to guide him in preparing to meet the most pressing needs of the parish this next year.

Just now almost every congregation needs to hear ethical sermons, perhaps after Easter, but other concerns are even more pressing. During the years prior to 1930, when there was an atmosphere of so-called optimism, the spirit of the preacher should often have been that of Isaiah 1–39, or else the Book of Amos, where the prophet is warning the people about the judgment of God on social unrighteousness. But now that doom seems to have descended there is special need of spiritual consolation, such as one finds in Isaiah 40–66: " 'Comfort ye, comfort ye my people,' saith your God. 'Speak to the heart of Jerusalem.' " [39]

In the normal church at the present time the most pressing need appears to be that of doctrine, evangelism, and comfort—comfort in the sense that good people ought to become strong in the Lord. But there is also a place for Biblical ethics. Where is the group of Christian people who do not need to hear popular

[39] Isa. 40:1, from the Hebrew.

169

interpretations of how to live for God amid these troublous times? So let every minister determine that under the guidance of the Holy Spirit he will learn to excel in the most difficult kind of pulpit work.[40]

[40] On the ethical question today, see W. L. Lingle, *The Bible and Social Problems*, Revell, 1929 (practical); A. D. Mattson, *Christian Ethics*, Augustana, 1938; F. G. Peabody, *Jesus Christ and the Social Question*, Macmillan, 1900; A. G. Widgery, *Christian Ethics in History and Modern Life*, Round Table Press, 1940.

Chapter IX

USING CHURCH HISTORY

AFTER EASTER ONE MAY HAVE A NUMBER OF SERMONS ABOUT church history. Such pastoral teaching usually comes at the evening service, at vespers, or at the midweek meeting. In any case, the emphasis is on biography. This is a good way to instruct new converts, as well as members of long standing. Apart from the Bible, no field is more fruitful, and no other is so little used as the source of materials for the pulpit. The difficulty is that a man must know the facts of history, and be able to use them in meeting human needs today. The best way to learn the facts is to single out a certain period, or else a character. If for a while one hesitates about preaching an entire sermon based on church history, one can use some of the facts in the form of living examples.

A SOURCE OF ILLUSTRATIONS

There should be a large use of church history as a source of illustrations. To show the influence of a godly mother over her son, tell about Monica and Augustine, Anthusa and Chrysostom, or Nonna and Gregory Nazianzen. A single example at a time is enough. Bring out the greatness of the man, and then show the influence of the mother. To illustrate the relation of a godly father to his son, use facts about the father of David Livingstone, John G. Paton, or Woodrow Wilson. President Wilson had studied under many learned and brilliant professors, but still he declared, "My best training came from my father." [1]

[1] J. Daniels, *The Life of Woodrow Wilson*, Winston, 1924, p. 27.

William M. Clow sometimes uses illustrations from church history. In his sermon on the Transfiguration [2] he is discussing "the blessing of the cloister hour," "the peril of the cloister life," and "the keeping of the cloister spirit amid the crowd." The chief illustration is a legend about St. Simeon Stylites, the hermit who kept his vigil on the top of a pillar. At last, under the guidance of an angel, the hermit descends from his pillar and goes down into the valley. There the "saint" sees a goatherd watching over a little child whose father and mother have been slain by robbers. In Clow's message these words are climactic:

O son [cries the hermit to the peasant], now I know why thou art so pleasing in God's eyes. Early hast thou learned the love which gives all and asks nothing, which suffereth long and is kind, and this I have not learned. A small thing, and too common, it seemed to me; but now I see that it is holier than austerities, and availeth more than fasting, and is the prayer of prayers. Late have I sought thee, thou ancient beauty; yet even in the gloaming of my days may there still be light enough to win my way home.[3]

An illustration may grow out of facts not directly religious. In his *Philosophy of Loyalty*,[4] Josiah Royce teaches that devotion to a cause requires more than obedience to rules. To a scene in the history of England the philosopher devotes four pages. In January, 1642, King Charles I wished to imprison certain members of Parliament. Not knowing how to apprehend them otherwise, he went in person to the House of Commons and there named the men he desired.

"Mr. Speaker," said the King, "do you espy these persons in the House?"

[2] Mark 9:5.
[3] *The Secret of the Lord*, Hodder & Stoughton, London, n.d., p. 227.
[4] Macmillan, 1908, pp. 103-7.

172

Falling upon his knees, the Speaker replied: "Your Majesty, I am the Speaker of this House, and being such, I have neither eyes to see nor tongue to speak, save as this House shall demand; and I humbly beg your Majesty's pardon if this is the only answer that I can give to Your Majesty."

The philosopher's use of the facts is worthy of note. At the outset he says that he wishes to bring the incident before the imagination. After he has made the scene clear and vivid he calls attention to the Speaker's act as an example of loyalty. In his attitude towards the King there is a blending of humility and unconquerable self-assertion, a willing and complete identification of self with a cause, and a readiness to die rather than be untrue to conscience.

Here is another example. One is preparing to preach about the influence of a good woman. For a statement of the facts one can turn to the writings of John Ruskin:

The best women are known in the happiness of their husbands and the nobleness of their children. . . . .

The soul's armor is never well set to the heart unless a woman's hand has braced it; and it is only when she braces it too loosely that the honor of manhood falls.[5]

For an example from history one can use what Macaulay writes about Queen Mary. As the wife of an alien ruler who was fitly styled the "Low Dutch Bear," she supplied much that was lacking in King William:

Her face was handsome, her port majestic, her temper sweet and lively, her manners affable and gracious. . . . . The stainless purity of her life and the strict attention which she paid to her religious duties were the more respectable because she was singularly free from

---

[5] *Sesame and Lilies*, Lecture II, "Of Queens' Gardens."

censoriousness, and discouraged scandal as much as vice. . . . . Assured that she possessed her husband's entire confidence and affection,
she turned the edge of his sharp speeches by her playful answers, and
she employed all the influence which she derived from her many
pleasing qualities to gain the hearts of her people for him.[6]

Is it any wonder that Mary's influence over William continued
mighty throughout the last seven years of his reign, after she
had gone home to her God?

In Macaulay's masterpiece the three sentences at the close de-
serve to be immortal. He has been writing about King William's deathbed, and his farewell to Bentinck, his closest friend.
At last came the end. These are the final words in *The History
of England:*

When his remains were laid out, it was found that he wore next
to his skin a small piece of black silk riband. The lords in waiting
ordered that it be taken off. It contained a gold ring and a lock of
the hair of Mary.[7]

Anyone who wishes to pursue the subject further should read
the sermons of William L. Watkinson, the English preacher of
yesterday, who was second to none as a master of illustrations.
While not profuse, his examples are telling. He is especially at
home in the realm of science, but he also makes use of history
and biography. In one of his best-known volumes he is illus-
trating the idea that what is little may grow:

When the father of William the Conqueror was departing for the
Holy Land, he called together the peers of Normandy, and required
them to swear allegiance to his young son, who was a mere infant.

---

[6] *The History of England from the Accession of James the Second,* Longmans,
Green, 1889, I, 681.
[7] *Ibid.,* II, 773.

When the barons smiled at the feeble babe, the king promptly replied, "He is little, but he will grow." He did grow, and that baby-hand erelong ruled the nations as with a rod of iron.[8]

In another sermon, based on a text about Hebrew history,[9] Watkinson is discussing "The Punishment of Evil":

Nature shows how the weakness of God is immeasurably stronger than men; so does history with equal clearness. The oft-quoted saying, "Providence is on the side of the big battalions," is one with an imposing sound, but it is disproved by history over and over. Some of the most decisive battles of the world were won by the small battalions. More than once has the sling and the stone prevailed against the Philistine army. . . . .

The all-wise God sits on the throne of the world, and we are often filled with astonishment at the insignificant agents with which Heaven smites its foes, and causes victory to settle on the banners of right and justice. The World's Ruler defeated Pharaoh with flies and frogs; He humbled Israel with the grasshopper; He smeared the splendour of Herod with worms; on the plains of Russia He broke the power of Napoleon with a snowflake. God has no need to despatch an archangel; when once He is angry, a microbe will do.[10]

Much the same note of assurance rings out today in the preaching of James Reid at Eastbourne, England. In his best-known book of sermons the chief source of illustrations is standard English fiction, such as Scott's *Heart of Midlothian* and George Eliot's *Romola*. But there is also a skillful use of history. In preaching about "Masterless Men,"[11] or the lack of leadership, this

---

[8] *The Transfigured Sackcloth and Other Sermons,* London, 1893, p. 117. The text is II Tim. 3:13.

[9] Jer. 37:9-10.

[10] *Ibid.,* p. 136.

[11] Matt. 20:6.

divine quotes Napoleon at St. Helena: "When I was in my prime I could get thousands to follow me, but I had to be *there*."

In another message, "The Triumph of Faith," the text is from Hebrew history,[12] and the discussion is about the national situation today:

We shall never get through till we all bring the mind of Christ to bear upon the situation. . . . . In 1652, when things were going badly with this nation in the war with Holland, the great John Owen preached to Parliament, "You take counsel with your own hearts. You advise with one another. You hearken unto men with a repute for wisdom, and all this doth but increase your trouble. You do but more and more entangle and disquiet your own spirits. God stands by, and says, 'I am wise also,' and very little notice is taken of Him." Does not that strike the note of our need? God stands by, as He stood by the Red Sea; God stands by. Are we going to bring in His wisdom, the guidance that comes through prayer, the faith that comes by seeing men and things with the eyes of Jesus? [13]

In short, the best way to throw light on a certain truth or duty may be to employ facts about a well-known personage, especially some strong leader in the Church. Ever since Pentecost the experience of God's children has afforded a laboratory to test the claims of Jesus Christ. Even if the minister is well acquainted with only a single period of history, such as the Reformation on the Continent, or the Great Awakening here at home, he has there an unfailing source of illustrations. After a few years of such preaching, however, he may wish to use historical materials more directly. Whatever the method, he should keep on stressing biography.[14]

[12] Heb. 11:29.
[13] *The Victory of God*, Hodder & Stoughton, London, 1933, p. 126.
[14] See *supra*, pp. 57-59, 171-75.

MIGHTY MEN OF THE CHURCH

We turn now to a series of historical sermons. The proposal here is to preach on Christian truths and duties as exemplified in chosen founders and leaders. At the Lutheran Church of the Reformation in Washington, D.C., Oscar F. Blackwelder recently had a series on "Men Who Overcame." The characters were Jeremiah, Augustine, Francis of Assisi, Livingstone, Sadhu Singh, Kagawa, Grenfell, and Schweitzer. Usually it is better to range less widely. But any layman who glances over the printed list will know that the minister has delved into books. Evidently the preacher understands why Thomas Carlyle wrote *Heroes and Hero-Worship*.

A more difficult series would be on a few fathers of the Early Church. A pleasant way to cultivate that field is to prepare three addresses, the first of which may be about Athanasius. According to Gibbon, "The immortal name of Athanasius will never be separated from the Catholic doctrine of the Trinity, to whose defense he consecrated every moment and faculty of his being." [15] The American churchgoer, however, is more likely to hear the pastor refer to Charlie McCarthy than to Athanasius. Any clever phrasemaker can prate entertainingly about a passing radio star, but surely Athanasius has had vastly more to do with the development of Christianity. In preaching about a historic character, stress the truth for which he stood. Augustine's doctrine was the grace of God, over against the works of man. He wrote *The City of God* when his world was in ruins and chaos. Chrysostom's emphasis was on the ethical demands of the Christian religion. These three would be enough for the initial series.[16] Whatever the Christian character, the suggestion is to show how

[15] *The History of the Decline and Fall of the Roman Empire,* chap. xxi.

[16] For a brief introduction see William Bright, *Lessons from the Lives of Three Great Fathers,* Longmans, Green, London, 1890.

a teaching of the Church became embodied in the soul of a leader, and thus helped to make him a power in the Kingdom of God.

Before starting to prepare the sermon, be sure about the facts. Know the character and the times. Read and take notes, as well as think hard. Be ready, if the need arises, for cross-examination by a lawyer who attends church at night. In preaching, however, the emphasis should be on the personage and his religion, not on the times and their spirit. The form of the sermon should be dramatic, not analytical. The discourse as a whole should be popular and moving, not scholastic and tiresome.

Such pulpit work calls for homiletical ability, as well as intellectual labor. But after one has learned how to use church history, one will find in this sort of preaching unfailing joys. One can follow much the same plan in a number of successive sermons, because the facts about the characters afford variety. For each discourse one chooses a text that was prominent in the experience of the character, and then one sets forth the substance of his distinctive message. One shows how his life was in accord with his belief. In the sermon as a whole, however, the emphasis should be on the truth rather than the person.

The message ought to be in a man's best homiletical form. The beginning may be about the influence of the man's mother, or about anything else that is worthy of note. For instance, take Luther's nailing of the ninety-five theses on the door of All Saints' Church at Wittenberg. There should also be a bird's-eye view of the man's career. Then in popular terms state the truth for which he stood, and discuss the importance of the doctrine today. Toward the end bring the matter home to the conscience and will of the friend in the pew. Throughout the sermon keep the hearer's mind alert and moving forward.

For object lessons of such pulpit work turn to *The Romance of Preaching,*[17] by Charles Silvester Horne. He shows how to make dry bones live. That is "The Miracle of Preaching."

LEADERS OF DENOMINATIONS

It is easier to prepare a series on founders and leaders of various denominations. One singles out bodies represented in the home community, whose ministers one can invite to preach. Since many churches do not hold services on Sunday evening, or in the afternoon, it is easy to secure attractive ministerial speakers.

In selecting the subjects, and in choosing the preachers, keep away from controversy. If any brother would be sure to come with a chip on his shoulder, invite him to speak at some other service, on the theme of brotherly love! After the denominational series, if it is a success, there should be an increase of good will among the pastors and members of all the local churches.

For this suggestion the writer is indebted to Blanton Belk, who when he worked out the idea was pastor of the First Presbyterian Church at Huntington, West Virginia. In a vesper service he would deal with the life and work of a church founder or leader. A week afterward a neighboring minister of that denomination would speak on what his branch of the Church stands for today. The series lasted fourteen weeks, which is much too long. Even so, the attendance and interest kept increasing, for the sermons and addresses constituted a novel study in the history and ideals of American Protestantism.[18]

The order of the characters may be chronological. If so, the series begins with Luther, and the pastor's message is on "Justification by Faith." The next character is John Calvin, founder of the Reformed Church, and the sermon is about "The Sov-

[17] James Clarke, London, 1914.
[18] See Charles R. Brown, *The Larger Faith,* Pilgrim Press, 1923.

ereignty of God." Then comes John Knox, founder of the Presbyterian Church, so that the pastor's topic is "The Kingship of Christ." In leading up to a study of the Baptist Church, one might deal with Charles Haddon Spurgeon, or else Roger Williams, and the topic might be "The Glory of Christian Freedom," or else "The Church of the People."

Especially interesting and timely would be the discourse on John Wesley, who stood for "The Eloquence of Christian Experience." In the message about the Congregational Church one could deal with Jonathan Edwards, or Henry Ward Beecher, and the subject might be "The Religion of Power." Among the Disciples of Christ in America the founder would be Alexander Campbell, and the subject, "The Church of the New Testament." The closing study might be on the Protestant Episcopal Church, with Phillips Brooks as the representative, and the topic might be "The Meaning of Christian Worship," or "The Glory of the Incarnation."

The series as outlined would last sixteen weeks, and that would seem interminable. If the sermons continued almost four months, the interest might wane. Where local conditions warrant, it would be better to deal with only four denominations. That would call for a series lasting eight weeks. On the other hand, each pair of addresses ought to attract a new circle of hearers; and if the messages are interesting and uplifting, many persons will attend every meeting.

Such a series ought to make clear the underlying unity of the various denominations. With the right sort of publicity, one can appeal to all sorts of thoughtful people. In order to do that, one needs to begin preparing months in advance. First one should be sure of hearty co-operation from the lay officers, as well as the neighboring churches. Throughout the series the aim should be to promote the Kingdom of God as represented in the local branches of the Holy Catholic Church.

HEROES OF THE MISSION FIELDS

A year later the plan may call for pulpit studies of foreign missionaries who have represented denominations at work in the community. On a Sunday evening the pastor speaks about a missionary hero or heroine, and a week later a minister of the denomination concerned discusses what his branch of the Church is doing in world missions today, or is making ready to do when the doors abroad are open again.

If this part of the proposal is not feasible locally, a missionary series by the minister alone would be interesting and helpful. In that case he would deal only with a few missionary heroes, one each night. Whatever the procedure, the series should be short. Unfortunately, partly because of wooden missionary addresses, the cause of world-wide Christianity has lost much of its appeal. But today, when reports of warfare in Asia and Africa and the islands of the sea have been schooling our laymen in world geography, missionary teaching in the form of biographical studies ought to be doubly effective. As soon as the doors into distant lands are open again, the Church should be ready to enter and possess each country for Christ.

A homemade missionary conference is in keeping with the approach of spring. During the winter the pulpit work has dealt with the claims of the Lord Jesus on men and women, one by one. Now there is need of training the new converts, as well as the other members, in the basic ideals of the Kingdom. By stressing the life and work of missionary heroes one can show that the cause they represent is the lifeblood of the Church. Instead of argument there should be case studies. There need be little mention of money, for that sort of emphasis will come more fitly at some other season. The addresses about missionaries should be informative and inspirational. The harvest will appear later.

The work of preparation will broaden the minister's horizon. Ever since college days the writer has enjoyed reading missionary biography. He supposed that he knew the field fairly well; but when he started to compile a list of founders and leaders in seven branches of the Church, he discovered that the majority of his missionary heroes and heroines represented his own denomination, and that most of them hailed from Scotland during the time of Queen Victoria. When he asked ministers in other bodies to name their heroes, he found much the same sort of provincialism. As a rule, it was necessary for the pastor to confer with the mistress of the manse.

The list as gradually compiled appears below. It is suggestive rather than exhaustive. Ideally, it should include a worker in every important field, and there should be women as well as men; for example, in Africa, Mary Slessor and Christina Forsyth. The suggested order is that of the seven denominations alphabetically. In the actual series one would begin and end with heroes sure to attract the people in the congregation, and one would shorten the series, perhaps by half. Usually it is wise to start and to end with representatives of one's own denomination. Especially in the closing study, the life and work of the hero should make the layman feel that winning the world for Christ and His Church is man's chief adventure here below. The title of the series may be "Missionary Heroes of Middletown Churches."

Baptist .... { William Carey, India
                     { Adoniram Judson, Burma

Congregational .... { Peter Parker, M.D., China
                       { Joseph Neesima, Japan

Episcopal	....	Bishop C. H. Brent, Philippines
		Wilfred T. Grenfell, M.D., Labrador
Methodist	....	Bishop W. R. Lambuth, Africa
		E. Stanley Jones, India
Presbyterian	....	David Livingstone, Africa
		John G. Paton, New Hebrides
Reformed	....	Guido F. Verbeck, Japan
		The Scudder Family, India

Every year after Easter there may be a call for a number of evening sermons, or Wednesday night addresses, relating to church history. As a rule one brief series in this field every twelve months should be sufficient. A young minister would find it easiest to begin with the leaders of four local denominations. A year later he could deal with the missionary heroes of these same churches. In the third series he might present certain fathers of the Christian Church, perhaps in the Middle Ages. The four sermons might be about Bernard of Clairvaux and Francis of Assisi, John Wyclif and Savonarola. By that time he ought to have learned how to use facts from church history in making a popular sermon. If so, his annual series will prove both interesting and profitable. Year after year the benefits to both pastor and people should be cumulative.

Whatever the special series, the work of preparing such messages should prove fascinating. The excursions into relatively unfamiliar fields ought to broaden and enrich a man's personality. Apart from the Scriptures, nothing else in the way of books is more rewarding than the best works of history and biography. Through such reading, month after month, a man ought to keep his mental reservoir constantly full. As a general guide in these home studies he may use the four volumes by

Kenneth S. Latourette, of Yale, *A History of the Expansion of Christianity.*[19]

When such pulpit work is well done, the benefits to the people are obvious. Historical sermons lead them into realms where few of them have ever ventured. Week after week they should learn how in crisis after crisis God has raised up first one leader and then another, girding each of them with power. Still other sermons, occasionally, may show how at times the Church has veered away from the ideals of her Lord and has lost her power with men.

Historical messages worthy of their high calling are energizing. They put iron into the layman's blood. Gradually they should lead him to a new conception of the Holy Catholic Church, a new zeal for his own beloved branch, and a new appreciation of the brethren who worship God in other ways. Where, save in the Scriptures, can one find a more fruitful field for Christian preaching than in the history of the Church?

Such pulpit work may help to solve the "Sunday evening problem." The second service affords an opportunity to inculcate the ideals of Christianity. In parishes here and there, men who are at home in the field of history have found that people are glad to hear about the past achievements and the present perils of the Church. If that is to be the effect of any series, every part of it should glow with light from above. The motive of the pastor, however, should not be to enhance his own reputation but to exalt the Church and thus promote the cause of Ecumenical Christianity.

[19] Harper, 1937-41.

HEARTENING

From Pentecost to September

Chapter **X**

MEETING LIFE SITUATIONS

DURING THE EARLY SUMMER THERE IS A TEMPTATION FOR THE minister to let down. After eight or nine months of toil in study and parish he is weary in body and spirit; he may even feel "all preached out." Probably he has no program for the pulpit work after Mother's Day, and no adequate provision for supplying the needs of his flock. Rare is the minister who plans as carefully for June and July as for October and November, or January and March.

A program may not be so essential in summer as earlier in the year. Before the coming of June the teaching ministry should be largely a thing of the past, and the sermons now may be more largely inspirational. Even so, if the minister forgets about his weariness and prepares messages of hope and cheer, he will find the pulpit work unexpectedly fruitful. In later years no part of his preaching will bring him more satisfaction in retrospect than what he does between Pentecost and the beginning of August.

THE NEEDS OF MIDSUMMER

In summer more than any other season good people suffer from disorders of the soul. When the worship and work of the congregation are at the lowest ebb, the layman is likely to be the victim of worry and fear, restlessness and discouragement. Just as these maladies are more active late in the afternoon than early in the morning, and at the end of the week than near the beginning, so are they more rife and pestiferous in July and August than in December and January.

For instance, take restlessness. While it may not be sinful, it makes a man feel wretched and lowers his morale. As long as he is restless, he may scarcely be worth his salt. If he can get away from the treadmill of the day's work, he will tear himself loose and hie away to the mountains, the seashore, or anywhere else, the farther the better. Because there are many of these restless souls, attendance at church in summer is likely to be irregular.

Here and there, however, one finds worship and preaching attractive to the restless man or woman. Such a sanctuary affords the sort of pulpit fare that one enjoys at a summer conference. A week at Chautauqua or East Northfield will show what many people like to hear in summer. At Chautauqua, for example, Albert G. Butzer of Buffalo recently spoke for five days on various aspects of "Religion and the Healthy Mind." James G. Gilkey of Springfield, Massachusetts, talked successively about "Winning Faith in God's Love and Care," "Managing Your Mind," "Making a Hard Life Easier," and "Conquering Anxiety."

Some of the other Chautauqua chaplains worked in much the same field. After two months of daily addresses by eight different clergymen there was no impression of monotony. At times, however, the speaker appeared to be more concerned about the diagnosis than the cure. Perhaps for this reason he had more to say about modern psychology than his mother's Bible. Consequently there was not much that would transform the life of the hearer. Doubtless the assumption was that in a secluded summer conference there is need of enlightenment rather than a change of heart.

In every home community there is more of a call for uplifting worship and preaching than in a cool summer resort. Especially on Sunday evening there should be such an opportunity. Two different summers the writer and his family spent July and

August in a city with almost half a million people, many of whom are Protestants. Sunday after Sunday the sojourners looked in vain for a church with attractive evening services. The places of amusement were crowded, and some of them were doing their worst to neutralize the influence of the Christian Church. But the doors of almost every Christian sanctuary were closed. In any normal community during the latter part of the Lord's Day there should be at least one house of refuge for the person who wishes to enjoy an hour with the Lord and His friends.

Whether morning or evening, the time of year lends itself to what used to be known as "the pastoral sermon." Of course every pulpit message by the home minister is pastoral, especially when he is meeting the needs of Christian believers. But in a more restricted sense the pastoral sermon is one in which he employs some portion of the Bible in meeting the needs of the Christian soul.

The current name for such preaching is "the life-situation sermon." Some of us prefer to call it "the message of hope and cheer." Whatever the label, the uplift of the hour in the sanctuary comes largely through the music and the prayers. In the atmosphere of worship the minister speaks from the heart to the heart, and thus he strengthens the soul in God. After many an hour when John Watson of Liverpool had spoken words of hope and cheer, his people would say to each other: "He puts heart into you for all the coming week." And yet late in life he wished that in the pulpit he had done more to comfort people.

This kind of preaching calls for a spirit of "apostolic optimism." The phrase is from John Henry Jowett. For object lessons turn to any volume of his sermons, or of those by Arthur J. Gossip, in Glasgow. Also uplifting are the messages by Leslie D. Weatherhead of the City Temple in London, and James

Reid at Eastbourne, England. Still more moving are the messages by James S. Stewart in Edinburgh, *The Gates of New Life*.[1]

Fortunately one need not cross the ocean to find ministers who make large use of "life-situation sermons," each man in a fashion all his own. From Pittsburgh, Clarence E. Macartney has sent out two volumes of such pulpit addresses.[2] In the elevator or on the street he overhears a snatch of talk that is characteristic of our time. Still more fruitful are the letters that come to him as pastor of a large downtown congregation. One of these plaintive epistles provided the introduction for an evening sermon under the heading " 'Our Friends on the Other Side'— When the Shadows Fall." [3] The message itself was about the communion of saints and the life everlasting.

At Hollywood, Louis H. Evans has been attracting throngs of eager listeners by his series of evening sermons, "Burdens that Bear Us Down." On the first page of the small descriptive folder is a picture of a businessman in his office. With head bowed down over his desk, so that nothing of his face is to be seen, his whole attitude is one of abject despair. On the second page appear the topics. Note the simplicity and clearness, for there is no attempt at adornment or camouflage: "Fear," "They Say," "Habit," "Loneliness," "A Guilty Conscience," "A Domestic Cross," "Temptations."

THE HEALING OF THE SOUL

During June and July one can deal with disorders of the soul. Sometimes the cause of the malady may be sin,[4] but that line

---

[1] Scribner, 1940; cf. his later book, *The Strong Name,* Scribner, 1941.

[2] *Sermons from Life,* Cokesbury, 1933; *More Sermons from Life,* Cokesbury, 1939.

[3] *More Sermons from Life,* pp. 189-204.

[4] See W. M. Mackay, *The Disease and the Remedy of Sin,* Doran, 1918.

of thought would lead us into deep water. At other seasons of the year there is need of instruction about the deep things of God, but in summer the call is for something with more appeal to the heart. Without delving into the mysteries of human existence here below, the minister can deal successively with the Christian cure for worry and fear, despondency and doubt, as well as other disorders of the soul.

While these complaints may not be matters of physical life and death, in the soul of the person directly concerned they often loom mountain high. If so, they are almost certain to prevent him from being useful and happy; they may soon weaken his morale and lead to a collapse. In such a state of mind, what a man needs from the pulpit, or somehow from his pastor, is a message about the Good Physician, who alone can bind up the broken heart.[5] That is why we sing in Charlotte Elliott's hymn:

> Just as I am, poor, wretched, blind;
> Sight, riches, healing of the mind—
> Yea, all I need, in Thee to find,
>   O Lamb of God, I come, I come!

In a thought-provoking book the celebrated Swiss psychologist, C. G. Jung, says that he has treated hundreds of patients from all over the world. The majority of them have been Protestants, with some Jews and only five or six Catholics, since most of them take their troubles to the priest. This is the testimony of the scientist, who apparently makes no claim to a religion of his own:

Among all my patients in the second half of life—that is to say, more than thirty-five—there has not been one whose problem in the last resort was not that of finding a religious outlook on life. It is

---

[5] See Jer. 8:22.

safe to say that every one of them fell ill because he had lost that which the living religions of every age have given to their followers, and none of them has been really healed who did not return to his religious outlook.[6]

As for the cure for such disorders, another thought-provoking book, distinctly Christian and evangelical, reports that a physician who is highly esteemed referred one hundred cases to reputable psychiatrists. His final judgment was that twenty of these patients had perhaps been helped, another twenty had been harmed, and the remaining sixty had not been affected.[7] What every one of those hundred distraught mortals needs is God. Fortunately, there are various ways of finding Him; for example, in personal conversations with the pastor who uses the Book and relies on prayer. But it should be possible also to find God through the messages from the local pulpit. If that is to be so, the man who ministers there should have a heart overflowing with sympathy. Anyone who has ever suffered from a nervous breakdown knows that the customary treatment almost everywhere else is sarcasm, and that it is refreshing to hear from the pulpit a voice of sympathy.

What, then, is Christian sympathy? Is it not the Golden Rule in everyday action? Pastoral sympathy means that the man in the pulpit keeps putting himself in the other person's place, looking at his world through his eyes, feeling as he ought to feel, and bringing to bear on the problem in hand some truth of God as revealed in the Book. When the minister has received this divine gift of sympathy, he can help to lift many a shadowed soul above these troubled sounds of earth and into that mystic realm where there is peace in the very presence of God.

In preaching about any disorder of the soul one purpose is

[6] *Modern Man in Search of a Soul*, Harcourt, Brace, 1933, p. 264.
[7] George A. Buttrick, *Prayer*, Abingdon-Cokesbury, 1942, p. 17.

to prevent many of those present from becoming its victims. Such an aim calls for primary emphasis on the positive, because the same kind of religion that cures the trouble will likewise ward it off. Meanwhile there is a tendency to linger over the diagnosis, which may not be difficult. Everyone knows that the occasions of fear have to do with sickness and accident, work and unemployment, money and poverty, children and others who are dear, old age and the unknown future, as well as the destiny of the nation and the progress of the Kingdom.

If a man is currently well informed, he can talk entertainingly for twenty minutes without even suggesting the Christian cure of fear. In his diagnosis he can employ the results of readings in psychology and sociology, as well as fiction and the drama, with many things else gleaned from contacts with the workaday world. Such provender may be satisfying to the curiosity of the hearer who is well and strong in spirit, but where is the Good News for the person who is weary and sick of soul? Is there no gleam of light, no ray of hope? Such a man in the pew yearns for help from the Living God. The need is acute, and it may be desperate. In the sermon, whatever the subject, the call is for faith. That means human weakness laying hold on divine power to supply a man's needs, for as soon as a soul-sick friend in the pew lays hold of the hand that was pierced, the healing in his soul is almost sure to begin.

THE SERIES OF HOPE AND CHEER

Sermons of hope and cheer are doubly effective when there is a series, which may well be from the Psalms. Summer after summer the pastor can take his friends into this mountain country of the Bible and thus bring them close to the heart of God. One advantage about such a way of preaching is that it gives the minister twelve months to prepare for each annual series.

A well-known pastor in North Carolina has recently taken his friends on such an excursion. Here is part of his report:

Last summer I heard you in two vesper talks, "God's Cure for the Blues" and "God's Cure for Worry." I thought that this would be a good trail for my outdoor vespers. So I came home and set forth. The trouble was that when I once got started the people would not let me stop. They kept suggesting additional subjects. But at last I am out from under the bondage imposed by the peripatetic professor. Selah!

The topics appear below, but not in the original order. If the minister had announced the series as a whole, he would have made it shorter, and he would have used the word "cure" more sparingly. If the reader wishes to prepare a series of his own, what should be the title? What is the best sequence of topics? How improve the phrasing? Such questions are technical, and are obviously of secondary concern. To them one should never allude in the presence of a layman. Nevertheless, the popular preacher devotes time and attention to details. He knows that the drawing power of a series depends in part on the wording of the general title and the specific topics. He wishes to give every sermon a name that will be attractive; he strives to make each message more interesting than the last; and he arranges to close with something climactic. In the printed list the subject might be "The Christian Cure for Soul Diseases"; the texts below would not appear:

The Cure for Fear ....Ps. 27:1
The Cure for the Blues ....Ps. 42:5
The Cure for Worry ....Ps. 55:22*a*
The Cure for Sleeplessness ....Ps. 4:8
The Cure for Indifference ....Ps. 85:6
The Cure for Doubt ....Ps. 73:16-17
The Cure for Restlessness ....Ps. 121:1

A year later the pastor can follow much the same course. In fact, if he will revise the list for each summer, and turn to a different part of the Bible for his texts, he can do this kind of preaching in the same pulpit for a number of years. From one summer to another he is addressing men and women who are afflicted by the same maladies of the soul. If he knows how to preach, he can tell the old, old story in ways that will seem new and wondrous. Above all will he point men's weary eyes to the healing Cross.

Recently a young pastor wrote about his second summer on the field:

What you told us about repeating the substance of our pastoral sermons is correct. I have preached a series of five "cures" and now the people are asking for more. The messages this year have been about anger, despondency, worry, fear, and doubt. In spite of what seems like covering the same ground as a year ago, I find that by using each time a specific passage, and not much else from the Scriptures, I can preach different sermons on any of these subjects.

As a by-product of such preaching, both minister and people should become better acquainted with certain psalms. Since many of them sing about the glory of God in the world outdoors, these inspired songs lend themselves to a series of services out under the stars. The general title may be "God's Songs for the Open Air." In each message the aim should be to satisfy the heart hunger of the average man or woman, and not simply to explain a passage. However, the best way to meet the needs of the human heart is usually to let the light of the Father's love shine out through a golden text.

Other parts of the Bible abound with passages that lead to

sermons of hope and cheer. At Orange, New Jersey, a series by Raymond I. Lindquist bore the general heading "Christ and Modern Moods." With a single exception the passages were from the Fourth Gospel. While the minister has done special work in philosophy and kindred fields, he is vastly more concerned about the appeal of Christ to the man of today. In the series all the sermons met with favor. The most effective were the second and the last, especially the last. The texts were not announced in advance of delivery:

Christ and Human Self-Sufficiency ....John 13:37
Christ and the Scientific Spirit ....John 1:46
Christ and the Evasive Heart ....John 4:29
Christ and Sorrow ....John 11:35
Christ and Doubt ....John 20:28
Christ and the Seeking Heart ....John 12:21
Christ and the Inferiority Complex ....Exod. 3:11

The introductory statement was simple: "Most of the Bible was written in hard times for dark moods. Its constant declaration is that Christ, the Son of God, can drive away the darkness, whatever its nature or its cause." In dark days the people should learn that every major portion of the Book was written by a man having a hard time, to men and women having a hard time, or about human beings having a hard time.

In days of trial and distress the Hebrew Church was cradled; in times of hardship and peril the Christian Church was born. As long as the pathway was rough the Church kept growing in grace, but when the world began to make the going easy for the Church she almost lost her soul. As Joseph Parker used to say at the City Temple, "Prosperity cannot read the twenty-third psalm." Now that his beloved meetinghouse is in ruins, those who have been wont to worship there can still find their home in God.

If the minister is to excel in such preaching, he ought to have the shepherd heart.[8] As he mingles with the people in their homes, and welcomes one after another into the study, he is unconsciously accumulating materials for his sermons. But in the pulpit he must be careful not to employ such facts directly. To no one save God should the pastor ever divulge what he learns in confidence.

Sometimes the temptation to relate one's pastoral experiences is almost irresistible. In a moving sermon, oft repeated, John McNeill, "the Scottish Spurgeon," used to chuckle as he told about a dying woman who whispered tᵣ him: "Dominie, dinna ye mak an anecdote oot o' me after I'm deid." The dear man was so impressed by her dying plea that he began to echo it all over the English-speaking world. But somehow he never became known as a pastor to whom the secrets of many hearts were revealed.

The minister who spices his sermons with illustrations drawn from his most intimate pastoral experiences may wonder why his friends almost never open up their hearts and pour out their troubles. On the other hand, in a vast city a clergyman can attract to his office a host of strangers who will be glad to take up his time and then hear him preach about their weird experiences. Of course every pastor should be able to "minister to a mind diseased." In his work as a preacher he can employ all that he has learned as a pastor, but the use of materials in the pulpit should be indirect and impersonal.

In warm weather the pulpit work should be Biblical in substance, simple in form, and attractive in style. Every sermon ought to be short, but not too short. If a man knows how to preach, twenty minutes or a little more will not seem long.

[8] See Arthur W. Hewitt, *Highland Shepherds*, Willett, Clark, 1939; C. E. Jefferson, *The Minister as Shepherd*, Crowell, 1912.

That allows a man time enough to make the chosen truth clear and luminous. He can likewise reach the heart, but he must learn how to select and omit. For example, in preaching about "Christ's Cure for Worry" a minister is trying to heal a quivering soul. Why should he endeavor to appraise the present world order with all its futility and despair? Without becoming sentimental or unintellectual he can be inspiring and helpful to the friend in the pew.

In messages of hope and cheer the faithful pastor excels. Thirty-five years after he had given up the active ministry, former President James McCosh wrote from what is now Princeton University:

When I began to preach I had about twenty carefully prepared sermons, but fifteen of them I could not preach. They were not fitted to move men and women, and I burned them. [The dear old doctor refers to the sermons, not the hearers!] I never learned to preach until I visited my people—the working man, the dying man, the grandmother. No part of a pastor's life is so rich in memories as those pastoral visits.

At no time of the year does a plan for the pulpit work bring more satisfaction than in June and July. If the minister keeps in mind the needs of people in the summer season, if he thinks about these messages from time to time throughout the months preceding, and if he works in the spirit of "apostolic optimism," he may do some of his best preaching when the weather is warm and other churches are either marking time or else closing their front doors.

> O Jesus, Thou art standing
>   Outside the fast-closed door,
> In lowly patience waiting
>   To pass the threshold o'er;

Shame on us, Christian brothers,
His name and sign who bear,
O shame, thrice shame upon us,
To keep Him standing there!

THE AUGUST SUPPLY

The effectiveness of the year's program for the pulpit depends in part on having the right sort of supply in August. We have been assuming that this is the time for the pastor's vacation. If so, who is to occupy the pulpit during his absence? Whatever the arrangement, the church should remain open. There should be as many gatherings in July and August as in October and November. Otherwise, any service that is discontinued will lose a good deal of its momentum.

The reference here is to the church school and the assemblies for which the minister is directly responsible. If these services are meeting vital human needs, there is a call for such a ministry in July and August. However, it is the custom to discontinue holding vespers, unless the services in midsummer can be held outdoors. Even there it is easier to keep up the interest whenever the pastor is at home and in charge.

In August the minister who leads in worship and does the preaching should be the best available. Those who come to church in warm weather ought to enjoy the most attractive fare that the lay officers can provide. In these matters the wise minister lets the official board do as it desires. But he should encourage the officers to plan for what will benefit the congregation. Sometimes, alas, the minister seems to be chiefly concerned about his own prestige; he may not wish to be outshone by the summer supply.

As a rule the pulpit fare in August should differ from what the people have enjoyed throughout the year. If the pastor is a teaching minister, they will relish sermons more largely inspirational. If he is a man of middle age, or perhaps older, they will welcome a younger man; the converse ought also to be the case. Whatever his years, the summer supply ought to be young at heart. The basic proposal at present is that in August there should be a change of diet for those who attend church throughout the year.

There is little to be said for the customary practice of having a different minister every Lord's Day. If it is impossible to secure the right sort of minister for more than one Sunday, that plan is far better than none; but such a way of supplying the pulpit leads to a lack of unity, and there is usually a shrinkage in attendance. Again and again experience has shown that with the right sort of man in the pulpit from Sunday to Sunday throughout August, or even a longer vacation period, the attendance is as large as during the last month when the pastor was present. When he returns in September, the people are ready to move forward.

Throughout the vacation period, especially in a congregation of some size, there should be a clergyman in residence. While the pastoral duties may be nominal, there ought to be at hand a minister whom the people know and trust. In order to meet the situation without extra expense, two local churches may join forces. At a county seat in North Jersey the Methodist minister does the pastoral work and the preaching during July, and then takes his vacation during August, when the Presbyterian brother assumes the dual role.

Another plan is for two ministers to exchange pulpits and parsonages. One may dwell in the city and the other in a village; one may live in the mountains and the other near the sea. For each of them a vacation means a complete change of thought and life, rather than a chance to rust. If a man loves to preach, he will find it no strain to share his thoughts and aspirations with the people of God on the Lord's Day. At a time when other men are giving their all for the country, the minister should set an example of willingness to serve.

In a large city church the pastor may be absent for two months or more. If there is an assistant who is able to fill the pulpit acceptably, there may be no need of help from without. Otherwise the engagement of the summer supply is a matter of vital concern. In one congregation the officers arranged with a seminary professor to live at the manse and occupy the pulpit. He also took care of the pastoral duties, which were light. The aim was to secure continuity of a sort not feasible when a different minister appears each Sunday morning and then departs as soon as he pronounces the benediction.

Somehow or other it should be possible for every pastor to enjoy new surroundings and cultural opportunities during his absence from the people. More important still, it should be possible for them to have the services of a resident clergyman who is gifted in preaching and in prayer. According to Arthur W. Hewitt, in his recent book *God's Back Pasture,*[9] such men are as likely to be found in rural churches as in any metropolitan center.

When shall we Protestants begin to take proper care of every local flock during the long weeks of summer? Fortunately the experience of congregations here and there shows that it is possible to keep the sanctuary open throughout the year. Some of the organizations may suffer, because the lay leaders are flitting hither and thither. But there is no reason why the quality of the hymns, the spiritual uplift of the prayers, and the inspirational power of the sermon may not be as pronounced as at any other season. Such is usually the case when the man in the pulpit has a soul burning with zeal to deliver a life-situation sermon.

[9] Willett, Clark, 1941.

If anyone is eager to start work just now on this kind of message, here is a good place to begin. The other day a godly woman, sixty years of age, the wife of an effective pastor, said to the writer: "How can I pray in a time of war? What should I ask God to do today?" That eager inquiry led erelong to a sermon based on the text, "Thy kingdom come. Thy will be done in earth, as it is in heaven." [10] The subject was "How to Pray in a Time of War," and the Scripture lesson was the heart of the Sermon on the Mount.[11]

Needless to say, in any such sermon the emphasis ought to be on prayer for the coming of God's Kingdom, and not on our winning the war. Nevertheless, there is a call for the use of concrete facts, especially from history. The entire subject proved to be fascinating to the preacher and of timely concern to the lay hearers. As for the permanent effects, they can be known only to God. Meanwhile the fact remains that there is today an unusual opportunity for the life-situation sermon.[12] Again and again, especially in summer, this sort of pulpit work may prove to be a very present help in time of trouble.

[10] Matt. 6:10; see Reid, *The Victory of God*, pp. 28-37.

[11] Matt. 6:19-34.

[12] For light on the subject from still other points of view, see R. W. Sockman, *The Highway of God*, Macmillan, 1942, pp. 118-26; also H. W. Ruopp, in *The Christian Century Pulpit*, May and June, 1941.

A FINAL SURVEY

Chapter XI

ADOPTING THE PLAN

FROM VARIOUS ANGLES WE HAVE LOOKED AT A PROGRAM FOR THE year's preaching. Now let us consider, positively and negatively, the merits of the plan as a whole. We shall view it first from the standpoint of the pastor. While the welfare of the people is of more concern, we shall think chiefly about the advantages to him personally, and we shall glance at some of the benefits to the congregation. Then we shall take up the possible disadvantages. All of them concern the pastor, for if he plans wisely and works in faith there can be no ill effects on the people, to whom a worthy program is a constant means of grace.

ADVANTAGES TO THE MINISTER

The benefits to the minister are practical. The plan encourages him to toil in his study five mornings every week. Amid parish distractions it is often difficult to concentrate on a chosen part of the Bible. But a man is always able to work hard on what he most loves to do. In that spirit he should approach the Scriptures. Instead of browsing here and there he can live for a while with Exodus or St. Luke, and later he can use it as the source of helpful sermons. Each year he can master a few major books, as well as other portions of the Bible, such as the Sermon on the Mount. In eight or ten years he can work his way largely through the Scriptures, and then he can fare forth anew, with still more zest.

The program likewise calls for the use of books outside the Sacred Canon. There is need of commentaries, works on theology, treatises on ethics, and all sorts of scholarly volumes.

Nothing of worth is foreign to the teaching minister. Morning after morning he enjoys his contacts with all kinds of books. In a sense he has to work under pressure, but he applies it from within. On the principle that a man enjoys what he does well, and does well what he enjoys, who should be happier than the clergyman as he lives amid his "friends in books' clothing"? That is no small part of what it means to be an educated minister.

> My days among the Dead are passed;
>   Around me I behold,
> Where'er these casual eyes are cast,
>   The mighty minds of old:
> My never-failing friends are they,
> With whom I converse day by day.[1]

As a motto such a pastor can take words that were written about a teaching minister long ago: "Ezra had prepared his heart to seek the law of the Lord, and to do it, and to teach in Israel statutes and judgments." [2] Another motto is from Paul: "Study to shew thyself approved unto God, a workman that needeth not to be ashamed, rightly dividing the word of truth." [3] These injunctions are especially for the young minister. After careful exegesis either text would serve as the basis for the charge at the installation of a pastor-elect.

A worthy program imparts to the minister's study and preaching a sense of purpose and direction. Instead of motion like that of a merry-go-round, there is progress toward a lofty goal. Everything leads up in turn to Christmas, to Easter, and to Pentecost. After that there is an opportunity to deal with still other matters vital to the welfare of the people. Without some high con-

---

[1] Robert Southey, "The Scholar."
[2] Ezra 7:10.
[3] II Tim. 2:15.

trolling purpose, much of a man's energies might be dissipated. In the study, as in the pulpit, one source of power is through limitation. If a man's interests were as broad and shallow as the Susquehanna River, his preaching would lack the driving power of a mighty purpose.

Long-range thinking encourages a man to cultivate the Biblical field from which he expects later to preach. Before he starts drawing sermons from Exodus or St. Luke, he wishes to live for a time in Egypt or the Holy Land. Since he cannot take the trip in person, he saturates his soul in that part of the Scriptures, and in related books, especially geography and history.

Such a method of study is like that of the playwright or novelist. When Charles Dickens was making ready to write *The Tale of Two Cities,* he transported himself in spirit over to Paris at the time about which Thomas Carlyle wrote his *French Revolution.* For months Dickens carried about with him a copy of that masterpiece, and erelong he knew it almost by heart. In various other ways he learned all that he could about those awful scenes, until at last he felt ready to begin thinking about his characters and plot. If any minister wishes to find joy in his morning studies, let him begin to taste the delights of thinking creatively. Then his sermons will become as inviting as the chapters of a first-class novel.

A worthy plan enables one to conserve time and energy, especially during the harvest season, when every minute counts. If for three months one has spent an hour or two a day in mastering St. Luke, one has found in it all sorts of seed-thoughts for future sermons. During the period starting before Christmas one can employ the passages most directly in line with the needs of the congregation. Meanwhile one can let each sermon keep on growing until it is ready to use.

Such a thoughtful minister is effective as a pastoral teacher.

Any teacher worthy of the name has a program for the year's work. Between New Year's and Easter, for instance, the college professor of Bible may have thirty periods of class work. If he knows the Book, and has a teaching mind, he plans to lead his pupils in mastering a certain part of Holy Writ. He devotes much time to mapping out his course, and before the term starts he has practically completed his basic studies. Unfortunately, however, the course may not be inspiring. In that respect the pulpit should not be like many a classroom.

The clergyman who plans for the pulpit is able to use in his sermons what he has gleaned from books and life. He can draw repeatedly from a reservoir that is full to overflowing. On the other hand, a pastor with limited ability and a narrow horizon may spend the first few days of the week almost everywhere except in his study. Then he is likely to waste the latter half of the week frantically scrambling after something to say on Sunday. If the cupboard is bare, how can the dear man hope to feed the household of God?

Time lost in the study is like friction in a machine; the energy is worse than wasted. Why, then, linger until Friday or later before deciding whether to preach next Sunday about the psychology of sin as it stalks through the opening pages of Genesis or the wonders of the New Jerusalem as it looms up in the last few chapters of the Apocalypse? Someday when one is working in the appropriate portion of the Biblical world, either of those subjects may prove rewarding. But when one does not know whether to preach next Sunday about the creation of man or the Day of Judgment, it is hard to keep from getting distracted.

The other day a minister of the hit-and-miss type declared that he almost hates the drudgery of preparing a sermon. He is a winsome fellow, but he has only average ability, with no background of reading or culture. Often he comes to Saturday night with no glimmering of a notion about what he is to say in either message on the morrow. Consequently his pulpit "talks" are thin and his people say that "he goes everywhere preaching the Gospel." Many of them like to go anywhere except to church.

To such a minister during his first charge a homemade plan would have been a godsend. At a conference of pastors recently a prominent Lutheran clergyman from Baltimore confessed that throughout his first year on the field he had stolen most of his sermons. But when he started preaching from the appointed lessons in the majestic liturgy of his church he was able to prepare far more suitable messages of his own. Erelong he began to regain his self-respect; he also learned to enjoy using the muscles of his mind.

At Fernandina, Florida, a few years ago when a young minister named W. F. Dunkle, Jr., became pastor of the Memorial Methodist Church, the membership was 181. Four years later there were 486. Meanwhile there seems to have been a sort of continuous revival. One reason is that the young minister plans all his work, especially for the pulpit. His methods differ ⌐omewhat from those described in this book. Fortunately there is no one stereotyped way of being forehanded in the study.

Constructive work is possible even if the pastor has no secretary or other paid helper. However, if there is a continuous revival the accessions of new members may lead the officers to consider doubling the size of the staff. Whether the minister has a number of salaried helpers, or none at all, what he does in the study and the pulpit must be largely a matter between him and his Lord.

In a congregation with a thousand members and a varied program there is additional need of a plan for the year's pulpit work. Throughout the main part of the year the pastor of our home church is busy about many things, all of them worthy. Morning after morning he toils in his study, joyously, because he knows whither he is going. At the end of a recent vacation, which included July and August, he said to a ministerial friend, "When the rush of the year's work is about to begin, it is good to know in general what I am to preach, and to have much of the material already in hand." Is it any wonder that he keeps on growing year by year?

At the beginning of the autumn this clergyman hands to the minister of music a copy of the tentative preaching program for the next few months. At her convenience she can select for each Lord's Day the kind of choral music that will be in harmony with what he plans to do in the pulpit. Especially throughout Advent both music and preaching help to prepare for the celebration of Christmas. Meantime she can be preparing for the still more vital period beginning with New Year's and leading up to Easter. Of course the minister of music and the pastor both understand that it may be necessary to alter the program for any week, but they do not find it difficult to change plans that already exist.

It is possible also for the pastor to select the Sunday morning and evening hymns, tentatively, two or three months in advance. The same is true of the morning readings from the Psalter, some of which may be in concert. Never until recently did the writer attempt long-range selection of hymns. For six Sundays in succession he was to be in charge of morning and evening services at a city church. After he had decided what to do in the pulpit, he chose all the hymns, and sent to the minister of music a list of subjects and songs for the next six weeks. Partly for that reason, the congregational singing and the special music proved to be unusually helpful. There was also a saving of time and energy for both the leaders of worship.

A still more fruitful suggestion comes from George S. Stewart, of Edinburgh, author of a stimulating book, *The Lower Levels of Prayer*.[4] He says that there are certain causes for which the pastor should intercede whenever the congregation assembles, and that there are other interests about which he should pray from time to time. The Edinburgh divine recommends that in making preparations for such leadership the pastor may work by the month, or even a longer period, so that in his public supplications there will be neither overlapping nor overlooking.

This whole idea of planning for the work of the pulpit is no mere recent Yankee device. In Great Britain some of the most honored divines have long found satisfaction in a popular teaching ministry. One of the most learned was the late B. H. Streeter, of Oxford, who vigorously recommended long-range planning for the pulpit.[5] Another scholarly English divine is Alfred E. Garvie, who has written standard volumes about theology, ethics, and homiletics.[6] Recalling the joyous days when he was a young pastor, he reports:

> To be a teaching ministry my ministry had to be a learning ministry. . . . . In the summer months, when the pressure of the work was less, I planned all my subjects and texts, for the most part in courses, from the beginning of October to the end of May. . . . . I did not waste half or more of the week waiting for the Holy Spirit to give me a text, but by constant study of the Scriptures, under the guidance of the same Spirit, I found more texts, the context at once suggesting the treatment, than I could use.[7]

[4] Abingdon-Cokesbury, 1940.

[5] *Concerning Prayer*, Macmillan, London, 1918, pp. 275-77.

[6] E.g., *The Christian Preacher*, Scribner, 1921—one of the most useful works in the field.

[7] *Memories and Meanings of My Life*, London, 1938, p. 128.

Any such homemade plan must be elastic. It should enable the minister to prepare in advance so as to meet the local situation. For instance, a young pastor in rural Maryland writes that between Thanksgiving and Christmas the worship and work are at their peak, but after the holidays there is always a lull. Instead of striving to change the prevailing trends, he plans to take advantage of the rising tides, so that his annual vacation comes in midwinter. For much the same reason, a pastor in a summer resort arranges for his annual leave of absence in October.

During his vacation such a minister can lay his plans for the next twelve months. He will find the undertaking difficult, for in some respects he will be a trail-blazer. However, he need not hold back, for he can seek and follow the guidance of the Holy Spirit. Otherwise how could any mortal dare to lay plans for building up his part of God's Holy City?

> Except the Lord build the house,
> They labour in vain that build it:
> Except the Lord keep the city,
> The watchman waketh but in vain.[8]

BENEFITS TO THE CONGREGATION

If the minister plans wisely, the benefits to the congregation are obvious. Whatever the local situation, a wise program for the pulpit enables the people to grow in appreciation and love of the Bible. Few laymen can hope to become experts in theology, but many of them are eager to gain a working knowledge of the Scriptures. When they come to church they should receive light on the Book, encouragement to read it in their homes, and guidance in living by it day after day. They also

[8] Ps. 127:1.

need to learn much about the Christian religion and the Church. In short, they ought to become informed concerning the meaning and glory of Christianity.

In due time many of the people will become enthusiastic about a popular teaching ministry, but at first the response may seem disappointing. Several weeks or months may go by before they become accustomed to the substantial fare. But in time they will discover that there is a new incentive for coming to church regularly. They will find that there is less difficulty than before in enlisting the young folk, as well as the neighbors and friends out in the community. When the people of God are sure to enjoy a wholesome meal, well prepared and served warm, they will bring others with them to the feast. Erelong the sanctuary should begin to be filled with the guests of God.

A teaching ministry also builds up the people spiritually. This is the thesis of Charles E. Jefferson: "When the sermons become connected chapters in a continuous story, the aim of which is clearly in the preacher's mind, the heart-life of the congregation is symmetrically developed and the parish is built up foursquare in righteousness." [9]

A worthy program also tends to make the people satisfied with their minister, as in many other cases they are not. By visiting among churches and mingling with laymen one overhears a vast deal of grumbling about present-day pulpit work. People say that the parson seems to be living from hand to mouth, and that ofttimes he misses the connection. Of course they may keep him busy all week running his automobile for the sake of friends who cannot secure tires and gasoline. Nevertheless, on the Lord's Day they expect him to deliver a helpful, inspiring sermon.

[9] *Quiet Hints to Growing Preachers,* Crowell, 1901, p. 93; see also *The Building of the Church,* Macmillan, 1913, chap. ii et passim.

In a neighboring congregation the visitor receives the opposite impression, for there is good feeling both in the parsonage and throughout the congregation. In fact, the people are tempted to be proud of their minister. They report that he reads and thinks; he prepares beaten oil for the sanctuary. He knows how to enlist men and women in doing the work of the parish, so that his hands are free for his high calling. Any such pastorate is likely to continue for years. With a clergyman, as with a suit of clothes, the question is, Does he wear well?

When the pastor works hard the people understand why he should have an extended vacation every summer. Meanwhile there is among laymen a vast deal of criticism about the length and character of the minister's free time. In two different congregations recently the officers have said to the writer, in substance: "Why should the parson have twice as long a holiday as any of us businessmen? He does not work half so hard."

In many cases the critics are mistaken. Nevertheless, there is a widespread impression that we clergymen are lazy. The laymen say that there is a lot of loafing on the part of their leader, and a loss of time whenever he tries to work. They wonder why he should need four weeks or even longer to rest when he has not done work enough to make him weary.

Elsewhere one hears a different sort of complaint: "Our pastor labors so hard that we have to send him away for a rest in midwinter, because we do not wish to have him break down just before Easter. But we learn that he takes his books along and studies several hours a day. Summer as well as winter he is the hardest worker in the congregation."

As a rule a month in midsummer ought to be long enough for a pastor to be away from his people. Those four weeks should be holy unto the Lord. For a lover of the pulpit the sojourn up in the mountains or down by the sea ought to be the most fruitful period of the year. Over in Edinburgh saintly Alexander Whyte used to insist that every pastor should have a long holiday. If a man never has time to take in, how can he always be giving out? Thank God for the person who devised the midsummer vacation! [10]

"There are men now fishing who catch no fish because they have never taken time to mend their nets." At the end of August, on the other hand, the wise pastor returns from his pilgrimage with body refreshed and vision enlarged through looking at life from unaccustomed angles. His mind is filled through varied readings, including theology and fiction, as well as poetry and biography. His plans are ready for the coming year's work, in both pulpit and parish. If that is an ideal to which few ministers attain, still it is good to have lofty standards for one's life work.

POSSIBLE OBJECTIONS TO THE PLAN

The objections to planning the pulpit work need not detain us long. Most of them hail from ministers who have never given such a method a year's trial. They judge it on the basis of other men's wooden performances. Really there is no drawback about planning as it works in the study of a minister who is wise enough to use a system without becoming its slave. However, we ought to note the most frequent criticisms, if only to guard against undue optimism.

First of all, planning does not suit every man's temperament. One minister thinks of himself as a teacher, whereas the neighboring pastor feels that he is a physician of souls. Where the teacher looks ahead and makes a plan for the coming year, the physician deals with each case as it arises. Meanwhile he may

[10] See E. H. Byington, *Pulpit Mirrors,* Doran, 1927, pp. 114, 137; Ian Maclaren (John Watson), *Church Folks,* Doubleday, chap. x.

not think much about the diseases that will be prevalent six months from now. "Sufficient unto the day is the evil thereof."

According to a recent biographer, Calvin Coolidge was

a far better man to do the day's work than to plan a program for tomorrow. He was no inspired dreamer. He lacked originality, the power to recreate and reorganize society. He was deficient in imagination. . . . . His viewpoint is expressed in a letter to a friend—"Let us all work together to get out of the present crisis, and not cloud the issue, or use up our energies thinking of other things." [11]

In the work of the ministry there is sometimes a call for a man of that type. If he does not build, neither does he tear down. But there is more likely to be a need of the pastor who can do long-range thinking. According to the New Testament, Christianity is largely a teaching religion.[12]

Since the man who has a teaching mind sets out in the fall with a definite program for his pulpit work, he knows what he hopes to achieve. He wishes to be as inspiring as possible from Sunday to Sunday, but he is even more anxious to build up the local church in the knowledge of the truth that makes men free.

Another criticism is that the teaching ministry calls for ability and training. Obviously this is true, but is it an objection? When God leads a man into the ministry, there is in him no lack of ability to do all that the work requires. However, there may be a need of training, for in college and seminary he may have been the victim of piecemeal teaching. In fact, he may have been spoonfed, much as a farmer's wife used to stuff a goose for a speedy sale. Even so, any man who is worthy to preach the

---

[11] C. M. Fuess, *Calvin Coolidge, the Man from Vermont,* Little, Brown, 1940, p. 497.

[12] E.g., Matt. 28:20; Acts 20:20; cf. W. H. P. Faunce, *The Educational Ideals of the Ministry,* Macmillan, 1908, esp. chap. viii, "The Education of the Minister by His Task."

Gospel can pursue a course of study at home. The work of planning for the pulpit calls for time and patience rather than brilliance and research.

A third protest is that planning requires time and effort, especially in August, when a man is all worn out. Even so, if his heart is wrapped up in his life work he will think about it occasionally while he is reading fiction or playing golf.

In the long run, planning leads to the conservation of time and strength. The investment of spare hours in July and August will enable a man to save his energies during the harvest season in February and March. Instead of letting his brains lie fallow throughout the vacation, he can start growing in his homiletical garden all kinds of seed-thoughts for future sermons.

The next criticism sounds more serious: pulpit work that is planned tends to become wooden. Ideally, the preacher ought to be an artist, not a mechanic. The sermon should bring a vision from God for the guidance of the friend in the pew, whereas planned discourses may seem like the blueprints of distant buildings. A vital preacher shares with others what he has seen on the mountaintop, but a man of another type assembles his sermons out of materials that he has previously stored in his filing cabinet.

The point is well taken. As an extreme example of wooden sermonizing think of the parson who prides himself on keeping two or three months ahead in his pulpit work. During August he writes out eight or ten discourses and then lays them away on the shelf to dry out. While he is using them he concocts a new batch. Whenever he takes down any of the stuff he has baked in advance, his people find it as uninviting as hardtack.

Such "forehandedness" is rare, thank God! The cause of the wooden quality may be lack of imagination, as well as common sense. Even if the materials were assembled and thrust into the

217

oven on Saturday morning, the finished product might still be unattractive. No way of working will transform a prosaic man at heart into a master of dynamic speech. What such a minister needs is not a program, but a passion, born out of imagination and heart power. "Lord, open his eyes that he may see!"

Much the same wooden quality appears in other fields of art. According to an expert in city planning, "The mere act of planning may be valueless, even harmful. . . . . What matters is not whether we plan, but whether we plan intelligently." As an example of a long-range program think of Washington, D. C. For a century and a half that fair city has been developing according to the plans worked out by Major L'Enfant, who in turn followed the basic pattern of the royal grounds at Versailles. Over in England architects have already drawn up the specifications for rebuilding the devastated areas of Coventry.

The objection, it seems, is not to planning, but to the wooden way it sometimes works. Without being mechanistic, the pastor who is forehanded is able to let each sermon mature for weeks or months. Whatever the period of gestation, he does not permit the message to assume its final form until a few days before the time for delivery in the pulpit. Then he should have back of him all the wealth of his experiences during the time the message has been maturing.

The last criticism is the most serious of all: the minister who has a program for his pulpit work is tempted to rely upon his methods and not upon his God.[13] Alas, that is true. But may not the other type of preacher also depend upon himself and not upon the Lord? Does not the Spirit of God work according to a plan of His own making? Is He not as ready to guide a man in August as in March?

[13] See C. H. Spurgeon, *Lectures to My Students*, first series, London, 1873, pp. 89, 99.

PRACTICAL CONCLUSIONS

A glance back over these objections will show that it is far from easy to plan aright. In fact, apart from divine grace a man's teaching ministry is doomed to failure. But why should a Christian minister not seek and follow the guidance of the Holy Spirit in planning the year's pulpit work? Again, why should anyone expect to excel in the most difficult art on earth without toiling hard day after day? In the Church of Christ during these awful times there should be no place for the clergyman who is irreligious or lazy. As a matter of fact, the two vices often go together, and the victim may be unconscious of them both.

If a man is spiritually minded and is willing to work, still he may not feel the need of making a plan. Not every worthy pastor is a teaching minister. If any brother feels that his present methods of study enable him to make the most out of his time and strength, that his ways of preaching are as good as God can expect, and that his people are growing in wisdom and grace, because he is providing every week abundance of Biblical food, why should he consider adopting some other way of doing God's work?

Perhaps unfortunately, however, such a feeling of satisfaction with present ways of working is rare among parish ministers today. Many a zealous pastor is conscious of lost motion in the study, misdirected energy in the pulpit, and imperfect fruits out in the field. If so, why not reverse the order of thinking, so as to start with the people and their needs? Of course one ought to begin with God, but under His guidance the order should be: the needs of the people—govern the work in the study—in preparing for the pulpit.

Here, then, is the heart of a popular teaching program: be a faithful pastor of the flock, a diligent student of the Book, and a helpful preacher of the Gospel. In order to do all that, a minister needs constantly to employ his imagination.[14] With God-given insight the minister who loves his people can discern the needs of their hearts and in the Book can discover the divine provision for all those needs. In the hour of worship under his inspiring leadership heaven and earth should meet together while the angels of God are ascending and descending with blessings from above. In other words, the man who preaches employs God's Book in feeding God's children.

Such is the ideal; it is also a fact of experience. Many a parish leader has found in a popular teaching ministry a practical means of harnessing together his pastoral work, his daily study, and his weekly sermons. With such a program he finds that all these things work together with a sort of "pre-established harmony." Not for all the world would one of these teaching ministers go back to the hit-and-miss methods of the days before he knew the joys of planning the year's pulpit work.

Such is the testimony of effective pastors all over our land, as well as across the sea. Since there is in many quarters today a desire for more of a popular teaching ministry, why not begin now to make a tentative plan for the coming year? As in every other sort of high endeavor, a man learns to do good work by doing his best day after day. Hence the second year's plans ought to be better than those of the first, and every twelve months should witness a growth in practical effectiveness, as well as personal satisfaction. In the right sort of teaching ministry the best is always yet to be.

Meantime the power remains with God. He is waiting now to bless everyone whom He has called into the ministry during these difficult days. The Bible is full of promises to the minister

[14] See Blackwood, *Preaching from the Bible*, chap. xiii, "The Interpreter's Imagination."

who plans his work in faith and then carries out his program with enthusiasm. Of the two texts that appear below, one speaks in terms of a rural field, with its changing seasons, whereas the other tells more about the city, where the unit of thought is the month. Either of the passages would serve as a motto for a pastor who wishes to use the Bible as the basis of a popular teaching ministry throughout the coming years:

As the rain cometh down, and the snow from heaven, and returneth not thither, but watereth the earth, and maketh it bring forth and bud, that it may give seed to the sower, and bread to the eater: so shall my word be that goeth forth out of my mouth: it shall not return unto me void, but it shall accomplish that which I please, and it shall prosper in the things whereto I sent it.[15]

He shewed me a pure river of water of life, clear as crystal, proceeding out of the throne of God and of the Lamb. In the midst of the street of it, and on either side of the river, was there the tree of life, which bare twelve manner of fruits, and yielded her fruit every month: and the leaves of the tree were for the healing of the nations.[16]

[15] Isa. 55:10-11.
[16] Rev. 22:1-2.

APPENDIX

APPENDIX

STORING THE FRUITS OF STUDY

THE PRECEDING CHAPTERS MAY HAVE SUGGESTED THE QUERY: "What should the minister do with all the sermonic materials that accumulate in the study?" While the matter is of secondary concern, it merits attention.

The obvious way to file Biblical materials is under the various books. For this purpose the writer would use manila folders large enough to contain sheets of standard size for the typewriter. There should be a separate folder for each major book of the Bible. After a few years there may be more than one folder for the Psalms, or St. Luke. Within each folder the arrangement is by chapters and verses.

At first a man will need only a few folders. In the seminary he can experiment with the sort of large manila envelopes that come with catalogues. The advantage in using folders permanently is that there need be no crease in any paper. There is also less difficulty in locating any item quickly.

In the course of time the minister who studies his Bible every day will have materials concerning each major book. Occasionally he will find elsewhere in print something that he wishes to preserve because it throws light on a certain passage. But as a rule he will put in the files the results of his own reading and thinking about Isaiah or Philippians.

The proposal is to preserve in orderly fashion all that one learns about any part of the Bible. For instance, one makes a careful study of First Peter, which is doubly precious in times of distress. The emphasis is on the Epistle as a whole, and then on the successive paragraphs. In the folder one puts careful notes.

The fact that one has written them down helps to stamp these truths on the memory. In later years one can turn to them as a source of materials relating to any part of First Peter.

Once again, think of the eighth psalm. At a young people's meeting one has just spoken about the Biblical teaching concerning man. In the folder marked "Psalms" one puts all the materials that one wishes to preserve in connection with the eighth. Years later when there is a call for preaching on the subject it will be possible to start with the results of this previous study.

The advantage in using folders rather than notebooks is that folders require less space in the study; also they are easier to handle separately. However, there is no essential difference between filing materials in folders and in looseleaf notebooks. As for the old-fashioned way of using books that are bound, there is difficulty in locating any item quickly.

The advantage in using folders rather than cards is that a large sheet of paper will hold as much material as a dozen cards. If in college a man has formed the habit of putting on cards the results of his reading and thinking, naturally he should not change the system. But if he is starting from scratch he will find it easier to handle eight or ten sheets of paper with materials about the Gospel of John than it would be to use the same materials when strung out over a hundred cards.

However, there is a place for cards. The writer prefers ones that are four by six inches; other men use those that are three by five. A card four by six inches will contain fourteen items. The main purpose of the cards is to catalogue a man's library. At first it may not seem necessary to show where among the volumes there is an important reference to the eighth psalm or the thirteenth chapter of First Corinthians. But as there is a growth in the number and variety of the books, there is value in having a topical index.

The folders and the cards should supplement each other. Together they should indicate the range and value of a man's Biblical studies, as well as his other reading and thinking. Meanwhile there are all sorts of materials that do not lend themselves to any such Biblical classification. For example, if the pastor has made a careful study of the Incarnation, or of church music, the obvious way to file the resulting materials is under a topical heading.

One of the folders may be marked "Biography, Non-Biblical." Apart from the Scriptures few books are so interesting and suggestive as standard biographies, such as *The Life of Pasteur,* by Vallery-Radot.[1] This kind of reading will be doubly profitable if one takes notes and then files them for later reference. For instance, from *The Life of Sir William Osler* [2] there should come several pages of excerpts, such as:

He was a rapid, methodical reader, with an exceptionally retentive memory. He had formed the habit of jotting down the gist of what he read, so that he could draw on it when needed. Moreover, he would augment the notes with reflections of his own. It was due to this habit of writing as he read that he finally acquired the charm of style which characterized his later essays.[3]

Osler himself said: "I wish that I had time to speak of the value of note-taking. . . . . Routine and system, when once made a habit, facilitate work. The busier you are, the more you can make observations." [4] Is it any wonder that Dr. Osler's reservoir was always full to overflowing?

[1] Constable, London, 1920.
[2] Harvey Cushing, Oxford, 1925.
[3] *Op. cit.,* I, 91.
[4] *Ibid.,* I, 242, 328.

The biographer does not tell how Osler kept track of the notes that resulted from his reading and thinking. Since he was almost a genius, doubtless he had a method distinctly his own. What concerns us now is that although his memory was phenomenal he made constant use of his previous notes. Whenever he started to write a lecture or a book he could employ the results of his earlier studies in that field.

The system that commends itself to many pastors is a combination of a filing cabinet and a card index. The cabinet in view has four drawers, the card index two. If there were need of labels—as there is not—the top drawer of the cabinet might be marked "BIBLE"; the second, "SUBJECTS"; the third, "LETTERS"; and the fourth, "SERMONS." Such a cabinet is warranted to keep a man's sermons dry! One drawer of the card index may be marked "BIBLE"; the other, "SUBJECTS."

The file and card drawers marked "SUBJECTS" may have such subdivisions as the following:

Arts, Fine	Education, Christian
Archaeology	Education, Secular
Baptism	Easter
Bible	Evangelism
Biography, Non-Biblical	Faith and Doubt
Characters, Old Testament	Fiction
Characters, New Testament	Forgiveness of Sins
Children	Funeral
Christian Life (subdivide?)	God (Trinity)
Christmas	Heaven and Hell
Church	Holy Spirit
Church School	Holy Week
Conscience	Illustrations (Unclassified)
Conversion	Incarnation
Cross	Lord's Day
Deity of Christ	Lord's Supper

Men's Work	Service, Christian
Miracles, Gospel	Sin
Missions at Home	Special Days (subdivide?)
Missions Abroad	Temptation
Money (Trusteeship)	Ten Commandments
Music, Sacred	Theology (subdivide?)
Nation	Vices (Seven Deadly Sins)
Parables	Virtues (subdivide?)
Poetry	War and Peace
Prayer	Women's Work
Providence, Divine	Worship, Public
Sermon on the Mount	Young People

The list of topics here is only suggestive. It shows what subjects were of special concern to the writer when he was a pastor. Any minister can draw up a list that will suit his own personal needs. For instance, if he serves in a body that stresses the historic Church Year, he may need separate entries for materials concerning Advent, Epiphany, Lent, and Whitsuntide. In short, the system is made by the man, not the man for the system.

This list is much too long and complicated for a beginner. If he is wise, he will start with a few topics and then add others as fresh materials call for additional headings. He will avoid having many cross references, which are a weariness to the flesh, if not an abomination to the Lord. As the number and variety of his resources keep increasing, so should his ability to find what he has stored. The way of working is like that of his mother with her jellies and jams. In March she has no difficulty in laying her hand on what she put away last August. Storing the fruits of a man's study is simply a matter of good homiletical housekeeping.

Such proposals differ from the counsels in books that we all

229

esteem.[5] Some of the most helpful writers on homiletics insist that it is better to employ one's brains and books than one's scissors and paste. That is correct, but why not use the brains in the study of the books and then preserve the fruitage? Of course no system is safe in the hands of a fool, but in the pastorate now there should be no place for a dolt. If it were feasible to take a ministerial census, few of the fools would be found with filing cabinets.

As a rule, the books about preaching come from men who are mature. They do not need many mechanical helps. After the first few years in the pastorate a minister can often go for weeks without turning to his filing cabinet and card index. However, there can be no objection to his using a system that calls for the preservation of what results from the use of his brain and his books.

The man who protests against time-saving devices is likely to have a phenomenal memory and a first-class library, with access to still larger collections of books. Probably he also has a private secretary or two, each of whom is an expert in filing and finding facts. What does such a ten-talent metropolitan divine know about the limitations of the average pastor's study?

The value of a minister's cabinet and card index depends on the contents. If the man in charge uses his brains while reading his books, he will gather increasing stores of silver and gold, whereas another man might collect a lot of wood, hay and stubble.

Apart from the Bible and the hymnbook, the most precious thing in a man's study may be his filing cabinet. If the parsonage were to catch fire, the cabinet might be the treasure most

[5] E.g., C. E. Jefferson, *The Building of the Church*, Macmillan, 1913, pp. 289-92; C. R. Brown, *The Art of Preaching*, Macmillan, 1922, p. 75.

worth saving. As for the card index, it consists mainly of references to a man's own books, and if they were burned the cards would be of little worth. But the cabinet ought to contain the fruitage of a man's reading and thinking about the greatest work in all our world.

INDEX OF PASSAGES FOR PREACHING

INDEX OF SUBJECTS AND PERSONS